AMERICAN BABYLON

Also by Richard John Neuhaus

The Naked Public Square:
Religion and Democracy in America

Doing Well and Doing Good:
The Challenge to the Christian Capitalist

The Catholic Moment:
The Paradox of the Church in the Postmodern World

Freedom for Ministry

Death on a Friday Afternoon:
Meditations on the Last Words of Jesus from the Cross

As I Lay Dying:
Meditations Upon Returning

Catholic Matters: Confusion, Controversy,
and the Splendor of Truth

AMERICAN BABYLON

NOTES OF A CHRISTIAN EXILE

Richard John Neuhaus

BASIC BOOKS
A Member of the Perseus Books Group
New York

Published by Basic Books,
A Member of the Perseus Books Group

Designed by Pauline Brown
Text set in 11.5-point Caslon

Library of Congress Cataloging-in-Publication Data

Neuhaus, Richard John.
American Babylon : notes of a Christian exile / Richard John Neuhaus.
p. cm.
ISBN 978-0-465-01367-8 (alk. paper)
1. Christianity—United States—21st century. 2. United States—Church history—21st century. I. Title.
BR526.N39 2009
277.3'083—dc22

2008047402

10 9 8 7 6 5 4 3 2 1

James Nuechterlein
Constant colleague and friend

Contents

AMERICAN BABYLON

I

Babylon Then and Now

THE TITLE MAY seem a bit melodramatic. Are we in Babylon? Are we in exile? Really? Speaking for myself, I know that a good many people think New York City is more than a little like Babylon, what with the babel of immigrant tongues, and the more ostentatious babel of sophisticates strutting their studied alienation from the America they have fled but know they have not quite left behind, and will never leave behind. "New York is not America," Americans like to say, and New Yorkers readily agree. "It's a nice place to visit but I wouldn't want to live there." To which the New York rejoinder is that it's nice to have them visit but they wouldn't want them living there either. New Yorkers tend to be that way.

While there is an element of alienation between New York and America, it is not in that sense that this book is described as notes of an exile. Anyway, I confess to being more or less at home in New York, and, truth to tell, to being something of a chauvinist about the city. I expect my friends are wearied of hearing me say it, but I have on occasion described the city—only half facetiously, of course—as the prolepsis of our hoped-for destination, suggesting that over the gates of the Heavenly City will be a large sign: "From the Wonderful People Who Brought You New York City—THE NEW JERUSALEM." One adds—with a smile, of course—that people who did not like New York City in this life will have another place to go.

The title of the book, however, is not *New York Babylon* but *American Babylon.* I am somewhat uneasy with that choice of title. Too many people, and not only Americans, are all too ready to identify America with Babylon. For people in some parts of the world, and not only among European intellectuals, anti-Americanism is a major component of their identity. It has been said that any identity is better than none, but that is doubtful. It is a pitiable thing to purchase identity on the cheap by pretending superiority to the superior "other," which is what America—as temporal orders are measured—undoubtedly is. America is Babylon not by comparison with other societies but by comparison with that radically new order sought by all who know love's grief in refusing to settle for a community of less than truth and justice uncompromised.

As for the *Christian Exile* of the title, it is exile from that new order. Exile suggests alienation, but this book is not an exercise in the literature of alienation that was so popular a few decades ago. With the political posturings of Jean-Paul Sartre (if not always his enthusiasm for political tyranny), and the polymorphous perversities produced by the "beat generation," sometimes drawing on the moral gravity of Albert Camus and with unearned borrowings from the existentialism of the much earlier Søren Kierkegaard, alienation was not so long ago the required frisson for admission to the company of the intellectually serious.

That is not what I mean by exile. Kim Philby, who in the heat of the Cold War ran a ring of mostly homosexual spies who betrayed British agents to the "evil empire," and who died an alcoholic in Moscow's tender keeping, memorably said, "To betray one must first belong. I never belonged." I belong, and I write for those who belong; for those who accept, and accept with gratitude, their creaturely existence within the scandal of particularity that is their place in a world far short of the best of all possible worlds. This world, for all its well-earned dissatisfactions, is worthy of our love and allegiance. It is a self-flattering conceit to think we deserve a better world. What's wrong with this one begins with us. And yet we are dissatisfied. Our restless discontent takes the form not of complaint but of hope. There is a promise not yet fulfilled. One lives in discontented gratitude for the promise, which is to say one lives in hope.

And so, in this book I depict a way of being in a world that is not yet the world for which we hope. This means exploring the possibilities and temptations one confronts as a citizen of a country that is prone to mistaking itself for the destination. It means also a cultivated skepticism about the idea of historical progress, especially moral progress, when that idea defies or denies the limits of history upon which our humanity depends. It means sympathetic—and sometimes not so sympathetic—engagement with some of the more troublesome, and more interesting, citizens of this present Babylon. The "new atheists," for instance, who are enamored of antique arguments that seem never to lose their seductive charm. Of most particular interest are the "liberal ironists" who take their cue from the late Richard Rorty, perhaps the most influential American philosopher of recent decades.

The argument is that everybody lives in hope, including those who cannot give a reason for their hoping. For everyone, hoping can't be helped. The Christian reason for hope is intimately, indeed inseparably, connected with the history of the people of Israel. As Jesus said to the Samaritan woman at the well, "Salvation is from the Jews." Understanding the implications of that truth enables Christians and Jews to live together not only in mutual respect and dialogue but in a shared exploration of our public duties in this place of exile that is far short of the final fulfillment of Messianic promise. Among the most glaring indications that we are in exile is the necessity of contending for the most basic truth of the dignity of the human person. If we don't get that right, we are unlikely to get right many other questions of great moral and political moment.

So hope is the controlling argument, and exile in Babylon is the controlling metaphor. Babylon is both ancient history and the stuff of tomorrow's news. The ruins of the once famous (and infamous) city are in the suburbs of Baghdad in today's Iraq. Well over two millennia before the American invasion of Iraq in 2003, the Greek writer Herodotus, often called "the father of history," brought the wonders of Babylon to the attention of the West. The name Babylon is a Greek form of the original

Akkadian name *Bab-Ilu,* which means "the gate of god." Both literally and figuratively, Babylon has been the gate through which many gods have entered history. Today it is Allah, whose more aggressive adherents are forcing the West to ask painful questions about who we are—questions about our God and our gods.

I note in passing, although it is a matter of more than passing urgency, that there is still today in Iraq a substantial Christian community. Until a few years ago, there were close to 2 million Christians in Iraq. Now only 500,000 or even fewer remain, and their numbers are fast dwindling. Most of them are Chaldean Christians belonging to a church that is in full communion with Rome. They are among the oldest continuing Christian communities in the world. Their history of almost 2,000 years includes 1,400 years of living in uneasy coexistence with Muslims after Islam conquered what had been a Christian society. Most of the Chaldean Christians of Iraq have gone into yet another exile in America, establishing strong communities near Detroit, Michigan, and San Diego, California. The safety of the remaining Christian communities in Iraq and elsewhere in the Middle East is a matter of pressing concern for the Catholic Church and has long complicated Rome's diplomatic relations with that part of the world. Those of us for whom Babylon is a matter of biblical history and religious metaphor should not forget the many Christians for whom Babylon is the all-too-frightening reality of jihadist persecution, extortion, and daily terror.

Most Christians remember the biblical Babylon in connection with the Tower of Babel. The story is found in the eleventh chapter of the Book of Genesis:

> Now the whole earth had one language and few words. As men migrated from the East, they found a plain in the land of Shinar and settled there. And they said to one another, "Come, let us make bricks and burn them thoroughly." And they had brick for stone and bitumen for mortar. Then they said, "Come, let us build ourselves a city, and a tower with its top in the heavens, and let us make a name for ourselves, lest we be scattered abroad upon the face of the whole earth." And the Lord came down to see the city and the tower, which the sons of men had built. And the Lord said, "Behold, they are one people, and they have all one language; and this is only the beginning of what they will do; and nothing that they propose to do will now be impossible for them. Come, let us go down and there confuse their language, that they may not understand one another's speech." So the Lord scattered them abroad from there over the face of all the earth, and they left off building the city. Therefore its name was called Babel, because there the Lord confused the language of all the earth; and from there the Lord scattered them abroad over the face of all the earth.

Babel and babble. Ever since, human history has been marked by confusion and conflict, with conflict, as often as not, resulting from a confusion of language. Language is more than words and rules of grammar. Language is the architecture and building material of the narrative worlds we inhabit. Without language there is no community. And the theme that underlies and weaves together the chapters of this book is that we human beings were made for community.

In the narrative world of the West—that large slice of Greek-Jewish-Christian history once called Christendom and not yet securely named by any other name—the name Babylon has powerful resonance. There is the historical Babylon and the symbolic Babylon. The ruins of the historical Babylon outside Baghdad consist of widely scattered tells, or mounds—some as high as 90 feet. There, too, are the remains of the city walls enclosing a space of several miles wide and several miles long. Nearly a quarter of the space was occupied by royal palaces and religious buildings dedicated to various gods, with the temple of Marduk being the most prominent, followed by temples for Ninmah, Gula, Ninurta, Ishtar, and Nabu. And, of course, there is what is left—which is not much—of the ziggurat of Etemenanki, once a lofty pyramidal structure with outside stairways leading to a shrine at the top. In fact, it is now little more than a hollow in the ground, having been destroyed by the armies of Alexander the Great in 323 B.C. The ziggurat was the Tower of Babel. To get to the top, the Babylonians went around in circles.

The historical Babylon gave rise to the symbolic Babylon. The Babylonian dynasty was founded by Nabopolassar 626 years before the birth of Christ and greatly expanded by his son Nebuchadnezzar, who figures prominently in the biblical narrative. (Some scholars call it the Neo-Babylonian dynasty because there was another one earlier, but that need not delay us here.) In 612 B.C., Babylon destroyed Nineveh, the great city that had been brought to repentance by the recalcitrant prophet Jonah. In 597 B.C., its imperial appetite whetted, Babylon attacked the kingdom of Judah and took Jerusalem captive.

The conquerors exiled many thousands of Israelites, including the prophet Ezekiel, and set Zedekiah up as their puppet king. That did not last for long. Eleven years later, in 586, Jerusalem was destroyed, Zedekiah had his eyes plucked out, and most of the Israelites who remained in the city were deported to Babylonia. The Babylonian captivity, as it is called, lasted until Cyrus of Persia conquered Babylon in 539 B.C. Cyrus permitted the Israelites to return and begin the rebuilding of Jerusalem and, most importantly, the temple in Jerusalem.

The Bible, both Old and New Testaments, is riddled with references to Babylon—to both the historical and the symbolic Babylon. The First Letter of Peter concludes with this: "She who is at Babylon, who is likewise chosen, sends you greetings; and so does my son Mark. Greet one another with the kiss of peace. Peace to all of you who are in Christ." Was Saint Peter, the first of the apostles, writing from the Babylon in Mesopotamia? It seems very unlikely. There is no evidence of there having been a church in Babylon at the time. The Jews had been driven out of Babylon during the reign of Claudius in around A.D. 50, so there was also no active synagogue, and the missionary activities of the early Church were largely based on the network of synagogues throughout the Roman Empire.

Recalling the earlier Babylonian Captivity, Babylon came to be a symbol of exile in Christian thought. Exile is a prominent theme in 1 Peter. The letter is addressed "to the exiles of the Dispersion." The author exhorts his readers to "conduct yourselves with fear throughout the time of your exile." Later, Peter writes, "Beloved, I beseech you as aliens and exiles to abstain from the passions of the flesh that wage war against your soul." The overwhelming consensus of the early church fathers and of contemporary scholars is that in 1 Peter Babylon is a symbol for Rome, and that Peter is writing from Rome. The connection between Peter and Rome was virtually unchallenged until the sixteenth-century Reformation, when John Calvin and Desiderius Erasmus tried to dissociate the apostle Peter from the papacy in Rome. Moreover, the Roman connection is supported by Peter's specific reference to Mark, who is strongly linked with Rome (see Col. 4:10, 2 Tim. 4:11), and by 1 Clement, a letter written in Rome in about A.D. 96.

In the last book of the Bible—The Revelation to John, otherwise known as The Apocalypse—Babylon is a symbol for a place or idea. In Chapter 14 we read, "Another angel, a second, followed, saying, 'Fallen, fallen is Babylon the great, she who made all nations drink the wine of her impure passion.'" Chapter 16: "The great city was split into three parts, and the cities of the nations fell, and God remembered great Babylon, to make her drain the cup of the fury of his wrath." And the next chapter: "The woman was arrayed in purple and scarlet, and bedecked with gold and jewels and pearls, holding in her hand a golden cup full of abominations and the impurities of her fornication; and on her forehead was written a name of mystery: 'Babylon the great, mother of harlots and of earth's abominations.'" And in the eighteenth chapter: "Alas! Alas! thou great city, thou mighty city, Babylon! In one hour has thy judgment come."

For the writers of the early Christian centuries, such as Augustine and Jerome, Babylon represented the power, arrogance, idolatry, and general wickedness of the Roman Empire. Also for Jews of the period, Rome was the new Babylon, for, like the first Babylon centuries earlier, the

Roman Empire destroyed the temple in Jerusalem in A.D. 70. For both Jews and Christians of the first centuries after Christ, Rome was the persecutor of God's chosen people and was destined to fall. Babylon represents more than the empire, the city, and the culture of the city of Rome. As one authority puts it: "Babylon is the sphere of idolatry and worldliness under the temporary control of Satan, a worldliness in opposition to the people and the work of God, a worldliness epitomized first by Babylon and then by Rome. Babylon . . . is the antithesis of the Church as the Bride of Christ, the New Jerusalem, and the Kingdom of God."

That understanding of Rome as Babylon changed over time. After the bloody persecutions of Christians under emperors such as Nero and Diocletian, there came a time of toleration, acceptance, and even triumph. Already by the end of the second century, the church father Tertullian sensed what was happening in his famous observation, "The blood of the martyrs is the seed of the Church." With the ascendancy of the emperor Constantine, Christianity was officially tolerated, and by the end of the fourth century it was the established religion of the empire. It seemed that Babylon had indeed fallen, just as the Book of Revelation had predicted, and Rome was on its way to being transformed into "the eternal city," no longer representing Babylon but the eternal hope proclaimed by the Church.

This triumphant reading of history was espoused by Eusebius, the bishop of Caesarea who is called "the father of church history." His *Ecclesiastical History* presumes to trace God's purposes—from Old Testament prophecy through New Testament fulfillment to the providential events unfolding in the fourth century. His *Life of Constantine* is a panegyric in which the emperor is depicted as the fulfillment of biblical prophecy in which the throne of King David is established forever. Today, and even in his own time, Eusebius' hyper-confident reading of history was widely disputed. The triumph that he celebrated is often derided as "Constantinianism," the precursor to centuries of "Christendom," and is frequently viewed not as the triumph of the Church but as its fall into a new "Babylonian captivity" in which it became captive to the temporal power it presumed to wield.

From the beginnings of the Christian movement up to this day, there have been endless disputes about what it means to say that Christians are "in but not of the world." All accept the words of Jesus that we are to render to Caesar what is Caesar's and to God what is God's. But there is continuing argument about what belongs to Caesar and what belongs to God. When Christian faith is most vibrant, the accent is on not rendering to Caesar what belongs to God. But there is no reason to doubt that those who, like Eusebius, relaxed the tension, and even conflated the realms of Caesar and God, were also acting in good faith. Over the centuries there has been conflation of church and state, coexistence of church and state, separation of church and state, and multiple other arrangements, none of them entirely satisfactory. The Second Vatican Council of the Catholic Church says that we should "read the signs of the times," and, in fact, Christians have been doing that since the time of the apostles and are doing it today. Different times, different signs.

The apostle Paul depicts the Church as being in a state of conflict with the temporal powers of the world around it. In the sixth chapter of Ephesians, he says: "For we wrestle not against flesh and blood, but against principalities, against powers, against the rulers of the darkness of this world, against spiritual wickedness in high places." It would seem that Babylon has not definitively fallen, and will not definitively fall, until it is finally displaced by the New Jerusalem of biblical promise. For the Christian, the warfare has not ended; we are still far from our promised home.

The New Testament Letter to the Hebrews dramatically portrays the continuing struggle of the saints who, because of persecution, could have no doubt that the cities of men were far from the City of God:

> They were stoned, they were sawn in two, they were killed with the sword; they were destitute, afflicted, ill-treated—of whom the world was not worthy—wandering over deserts and mountains and in dens and caves of the earth. And all these, though well attested by their faith, did not receive what was promised, since God had foreseen something better for us, that apart from us they should not be made perfect. . . . But you have come to Mount Zion and to the city of the living God, the heavenly Jerusalem, and to innumerable angels in festal gathering, and to the assembly of the first-born who are enrolled in heaven, and to a judge who is God of all, and to the spirits of just men made perfect, and to Jesus, the mediator of a new covenant, and to the sprinkled blood that speaks more graciously than the blood of Abel. . . . For here we have no lasting city, but we seek the city that is to come.

Note the tension. We might call it the dialectic. Some see it as a contradiction. On the one hand, we have come to Mount Zion, the New Jerusalem. On the other, we have here no lasting city but seek the city that is to come. This is frequently described as the "now" and "not yet" of Christian existence. Christians live "between the times"—meaning between the time of Christ's resurrection victory and the time of its cosmic fulfillment in the coming of the promised Kingdom. All time is time toward home, time toward our true home in the New Jerusalem.

And so it is said that there is a continuing tension between the "this-worldly" and the "other-worldly" dimensions of Christian existence. Some Christians put the accent on their duties to making this world a better place to live, to making this world more home-like, so to speak. There are even those called postmillennialists who believe that Christ will not return in glory until we have established a millennium of justice and peace, making the world worthy of his kingly rule. This has at times in Christian history, and not least in the history of Christianity in America, served as a powerful incentive for social and political activism on the part of Christians. In this view, it is as though we really can turn Babylon into the New Jerusalem by means of radical reform.

There is good reason, however, to question the ways in which this-worldly Christianity is pitted against other-worldly Christianity. Other-worldliness is often derided as escapism from the problems and tasks of the here and now. It is, according to many critics, a piety focused on "pie in the sky in the sweet bye and bye." One thinks of the old hymn, "I'm but a stranger here /

Heaven is my home." We should at least entertain the possibility, however, that other-worldly hope can intensify one's engagement in the responsibilities for this world. The *other* in other-worldly is not entirely other. It can be anticipated in this world fulfilled and transformed, at least in part. In this world that is worthy of our love and allegiance, we are prepared for what is to be. The Book of Revelation speaks of a new heaven and a new earth in which those who are faithful in their time are at last at home:

> *They shall hunger no more, neither thirst any more;*
> *the sun shall not strike them, nor any scorching heat.*
> *For the Lamb in the midst of the throne will be their shepherd,*
> *and he will guide them to springs of living water;*
> *and God will wipe away every tear from their eyes.*

Even in the Babylon of the present, the New Jerusalem that "comes down from above" is anticipated. The word for this is *prolepsis,* an act in which a hoped-for future is already present. The entirety of Christian existence and of our efforts in this world can thus be understood as proleptic.

For Christians, the supreme act of prolepsis is the Eucharist, in which we take bread and wine in obedience to the command of Jesus and "do this" in remembrance of him. Thus is the Eucharist, in the words of the Second Vatican Council, the "source and summit" of the Church's life. It is a supremely *political* action in which the heavenly *polis* is made present in time. The eucharistic meal here and now anticipates, makes present, the New Jerusalem's eternal Feast of the Lamb. So it is that in the eucharistic liturgy Christians say that they join their song to that of "the angels and archangels and all the company of heaven" around the throne of the Lamb, meaning Christ the Lamb of God who was sacrificed for our salvation. In this act, past and future are *now* because, as the Lamb says of himself, "I am the Alpha and Omega, the first and the last, the beginning and the end." Christ is the A and the Z of the human alphabet construed to tell the story of the world.

In this understanding, it is not a matter of "balancing" the other-worldly against the this-worldly, or the this-worldly against the other-worldly. Each world penetrates the other. The present is, so to speak, pregnant with the promised future. "The world is charged with the grandeur of God," declares the poet Gerard Manley Hopkins. Charged as in electrically charged; the present is given new urgency, raised to a new level of intensity, because it is riddled through and through with what is to be.

And yet, the "not yet" weighs heavily in the Christian understanding of our place and time in the earthly city. Babylon has not yet been displaced by the New Jerusalem. The early Christian writers embraced the understanding of the Old Testament prophet Jeremiah. Yes, a new world has begun with the resurrection of Jesus, but the "principalities and powers" still rage against the new order that has been inaugurated. No flights of other-worldly piety, no "raised consciousness" of the gnostics, provides escape from the burdens and duties of the present. According to Jeremiah, it is the God of Israel who has sent his people into exile from Jerusalem to Babylon. Writing in the sixth century B.C., Jeremiah counsels the exiles:

> Build houses and live in them; plant gardens and eat their produce. Take wives and have sons and daughters; take wives for your sons, and give your daughters in marriage, that they may bear sons and daughters; multiply there, and do not decrease. But seek the welfare of the city where I have sent you into exile, and pray to the Lord on its behalf, for in its welfare you will find your welfare.

Exile remains exile, and Babylon remains Babylon, but both are penetrated, both are charged, by the promise of deliverance. For Old Testament Israel, deliverance is understood as return and the rebuilding of Jerusalem. For New Testament Israel, deliverance is arrival at the destination of the long pilgrimage toward the New Jerusalem.

The Christian language of exile and return is drawn from the Old Testament. And so also is the language of a final destination, a language that is not limited to return and restoration. A hundred years before Jeremiah, the prophet Isaiah wrote of what "will come to pass in the latter days." There will appear one upon whom the Spirit of the Lord will rest, and he will establish a kingdom such as has never been before. In that kingdom,

The wolf shall dwell with the lamb,
and the leopard shall lie down with the kid,
and the calf and the lion and the fatling together,
and a little child shall lead them.
The cow and the bear shall feed;
their young shall lie down together;
and the lion shall eat straw like the ox.
The suckling child shall play over the hole of the asp,

and the weaned child shall put his hand on the adder's den.
They shall not hurt or destroy
in all my holy mountain;
for the earth shall be full of the knowledge of the Lord
as the waters cover the sea.

Obviously, this passage envisions more than a return to Jerusalem and the restoration of the city that was. And yet, the city that was and the city that now is is the prolepsis of what is to be. The promise of what is to be—the other-worldly, if you will—intensifies the devotion to the earthly city. Psalm 137 is among the most moving expressions of this sense of exile and return, of loss and hope, of sorrow and trust:

By the waters of Babylon,
there we sat down and wept,
when we remembered Zion.
On the willows there
we hung up our lyres.
For there our captors
required of us songs,
and our tormentors mirth, saying
"Sing us the songs of Zion."
How shall we sing the Lord's song
in a foreign land?
If I forget you, O Jerusalem,
let my right hand wither!
Let my tongue cleave to the roof of my mouth
if I do not remember you,
if I do not set Jerusalem
above my highest joy!

The psalmist cannot sing the songs of Zion in a foreign land, and yet he cannot *not* sing the songs of Zion, even though in a foreign land. This is evident in his singing the song of Zion that is Psalm 137. His singing of this song of Zion intensifies the awareness of being in a foreign land, even as it is hope's participation, however partial and preliminary, in a world elsewhere.

Meanwhile, we seek the peace of the city of our exile. The story told in the Old Testament Book of Daniel is instructive. When in 605 B.C. Nebuchadnezzar moved against Judah, he demanded tokens of submission, including young men from the royal and noble families. Among these were Daniel, Hananiah, Mishael, and Azariah. Their captors gave them Babylonian names: Belteshazzar, Shadrach, Meshach, and Abednego. The young men went along with that, although I expect that in private they called one another by the old names. Those old names meant something. For instance, Daniel means "God is my judge," while Belteshazzar refers to a goddess who protects the king. They went along with a lot of things. We are told that they were educated for three years in the lore of Babylon. This would involve learning the very difficult Akkadian language and studying the Babylonian creation and flood stories, along with how to tell the future by observing the stars, discerning the patterns of oil in water, reading the spots on sheep livers, and the like. After all, they were being trained to serve as Babylonian wise men. They succeeded so well in the ways of Babylon that the king made them governors of the empire's several provinces.

But there was a limit to their going along. We read in Chapter 3 the announcement by the herald of the king: "You are commanded, O people, nations, and languages, that when you hear the sound of the horn, pipe, lyre, trigon, harp, bagpipe, and every kind of music, you are to fall down and worship the golden image that King Nebuchadnezzar has set up; and whoever does not fall down and worship shall immediately be cast into a burning fiery furnace."

When the king heard that the young Judeans had refused to fall down and worship the golden image, he had them brought before him and declared, "If you do not worship, you shall immediately be cast into a burning fiery furnace; and who is the god that will deliver you out of my hands?" Shadrach, Meshach, and Abednego responded: "O Nebuchadnezzar, we have no need to answer you in this matter. If it be so, our God whom we serve is able to deliver us from the burning fiery furnace; and he will deliver us out of your hand, O king. But if not, be it known to you, O king, that we will not serve your gods or worship the golden image you have set up."

The king was "full of fury" and ordered that the fiery furnace be heated seven times hotter. It was so hot that the guards who threw Shadrach, Meshach, and Abednego into the flames died of the heat. From a safe distance, the king saw not three but four men walking in the flames and exclaimed, "The appearance of the fourth is like a son of the gods." He called Shadrach, Meshach, and Abednego to come out of the furnace and they emerged unharmed. Upon seeing this, the king cried: "Blessed be the God of Shadrach, Meshach, and Abednego who has sent his angel and delivered his servants who trusted in him, and set at nought the king's command, and yielded up their bodies rather than serve and worship any god except their own God."

Then the king issued a decree that terrible things would be done to anyone who spoke against their God, and he promoted the three to new positions of authority in Babylon. A dramatic tale with a happy ending, we might well say, and it is that. Beyond that, however, the story illustrates what it means to seek the peace of the city of our exile. The young Judeans went along with a great deal but drew the line at worshipping a false god. Much better to die than to violate the first commandment of the Decalogue, "You shall worship the Lord your God and him only shall you serve."

In the first centuries of the Christian movement, martyrs went singing to their deaths rather than do something so seemingly innocuous as burning a pinch of incense before the statues of emperors who had been officially deified. Also today, Christians worry about the ways in which accommodation to this foreign city can become betrayal. At least they should. The temptation to worship false gods usually presents itself in subtle forms. It does not usually announce itself with the sound of the horn, pipe, lyre, trigon, harp, bagpipe, and every kind of music.

Such are the uncertainties, and the awesome stakes, in this dialectic, this complex back-and-forth of remembering and anticipation; of living the brief moment of what *is* between what *was* and what *is to be,* never losing sight of a destination that transcends history but does not leave history behind. The "new heaven and new earth" of the Book of Revelation does not abandon *this* heaven and *this* earth. Rather, they are taken up into transcendent fulfillment. It is not as though this earthly city grows and develops into the heavenly city, the New Jerusalem. It is not a matter of historical progress but of eschatological promise.

Eschatology refers to the last things, the final things, the ultimate destination of the story of God's dealings with the world of his creation. In the Christian view, that destination, that *eschaton,* has already appeared within history in the resurrection of Jesus from the dead. As the New Testament scholar N. T. Wright nicely puts it, the resurrection of the crucified Jesus is not a story about a happy ending but about a new beginning. In the resurrection and in the abiding presence of the resurrected Lord in his body, the Church, the absolute future breaks into present time. Because the principalities and powers rage against the new world order inaugurated by the resurrection of Jesus, that future is discernible only by faith. In the words of Saint Paul, "We walk by faith, not by sight." That Jesus was raised from the dead is convincingly demonstrated as historical fact; accepting the implications of that fact is to walk by faith.

Christians do not—or at least they should not—claim to understand the intricacies of God's workings in time and through time. The details of the working out of the relationship between the immanent—the here and now—and the transcendent are not within our human competence. The Christian claim is that God—the Absolute, Being Itself, the Source and End of all that is—has invested himself in the human project. This happened in the Incarnation, when the Creator, the Second Person of the Holy Trinity, became a creature in Jesus the son of Mary, a truth vindicated in the resurrection of the Son of God. God's investment is irrevocable, and therefore the human project cannot fail, not finally.

Obviously, we're into deep theological waters here. What Christians can say about the particulars of God's purposes in history leaves us stuttering and tongue-tied. We can attend closely to what is revealed; we can try to read "the signs of the times"; we can study, discuss, debate, speculate, and then pray for the grace to act in the courage of our uncertainties. But at the end of the day, we say with Paul, "Now we see in a mirror dimly, but then face to face. Now I know in part; then I shall know fully, even as I have been fully known." These are words from Paul's unsurpassable hymn of love in 1 Corinthians 13. We walk by faith in faith's disposition toward the future, which is hope, relying on the cosmic triumph of the love revealed in Jesus Christ. Thus Paul's conclusion: "So faith, hope, love abide, these three; but the greatest of these is love."

What an extraordinary mix! The now and the not yet, the this-worldly and the other-worldly, the transcendent and the immanent, promise and fulfillment, time and eternity, time toward home and the prolepsis of home in time. That mix is both the burden and the grace to bear the burden of pilgrimage. The People of God is a pilgrim people. As Israel is a pilgrim people, so it is said in the eucharistic prayer of the Mass, "Strengthen in faith and love your pilgrim Church on earth."

In the chapters that follow, there will be occasional reference to *City of God* by Saint Augustine of Hippo. The references are occasional, the influence is pervasive. Writing in the fourth and fifth centuries, the bishop of Hippo Regius, located in what is now Algeria, wrote the story of the world, from creation to eschaton, in terms of the contrast and conflict between the City of God and the "city of man" or "the earthly city."

The earthly city of Augustine's time was the Roman Empire. The earthly city to which this book attends is chiefly, but by no means only, America. Augustine's *City of God* provides a conceptual framework. Literary critics speak of an "inhabitable narrative," which catches the matter nicely. For Augustine, the biblical narrative provides the drama of which we are part. *City of God* weaves into that narrative Augustine's penetrating insights into the possibilities and limits of the human condition. He is a master of subtlety in analyzing the desires, both rightly and wrongly ordered, of the human heart. He provides arguments, interpretations, principles, and rules, but—and this is most important—one derives from his writings what is best described as an "Augustinian sensibility." It is the sensibility of the pilgrim through time who resolutely resists the temptation to despair in the face of history's disappointments and tragedies, and just as resolutely declines the delusion of having arrived at history's end.

This sensibility builds on Peter's understanding of Christians as "aliens and exiles." It is a way of being in the world but not of the world that is finely expressed in *The Letter to Diognetus*. The letter was written by a Christian, possibly toward the end of the first century, to Diognetus, a pagan who was curious about the way Christians thought of their place in the world. The author explains: "Though they are residents at home in their own countries, their behavior there is more like that of transients; they take their full part as citizens, but they also submit to anything and everything as if they were aliens. For them, any foreign country is a homeland, and any homeland is a foreign country."

The author goes on to point out that Christians reject certain practices of the Roman world. For instance, they refuse to abort their children or to practice infanticide by exposing their children to the elements, as was common among the Romans. Christians recognize, says the letter writer, that they are viewed as alien, and are not intimidated by that. On the contrary, they rejoice in it. As the soul is to the body, so are Christians to the world. As *The Letter to Diognetus* puts it, "The soul is captive to the body, yet it holds the body together. So Christians are held captive to the world, and yet they hold the world together." And that is because they are the bearers of the true story of the world, whether the world wants to know it or not.

The title *American Babylon* will likely puzzle, and even offend, some readers. There is in America a strong current of Christian patriotism in which "God and country" falls trippingly from the tongue. Indeed, God and country are sometimes conflated in a single allegiance that permits no tension, never mind conflict, between the two.

I would be disappointed if readers did not recognize that this book is animated by a deep and lively patriotism. I have considerable sympathy for Abraham Lincoln's observation that, among the political orders of the earthly city, America is "the last, best, hope of mankind." Although it was added late to the Pledge of Allegiance, the affirmation that we are a nation "under God" is not unimportant. It does not mean that we are God's chosen nation—and we should be uneasy even with Lincoln's sharply modified claim that we are an "almost chosen" people. Nor does it mean that we are immune to the temptations and tragedies of all earthly orders. To say that we are a nation under God is to say, first and most importantly, that we are a nation under transcendent judgment. Judgment and promise are inseparable.

People speak of a "critical patriotism," and certainly patriotism should not be unthinking. But with critical patriotism it sometimes seems that the adjective overwhelms the noun. The result is a contingent devotion—devotion to one's country if only one's country were a different country than it is—which is no patriotism at all. The noted poet of the early twentieth century, Richard Wilbur, strikes a balance between criticism and devotion when he invokes the memory of those who have gone before:

Whose minds went dark at the edge of a field,
In the muck of a trench, on the beachhead sand,
In a blast amidships, a burst in the air. . . .
Grieve for the ways in which we betrayed them,
How we robbed their graves of a reason to die:
The tribes pushed west, and the treaties broken,
The image of God on the auction block,
The Immigrant scorned, and the striker beaten.
The vote denied to liberty's daughters.

Nonetheless:

From all that has shamed us, what can we salvage?
Be proud at least that we know we were wrong,

That we need not lie, that our books are open,
Praise to this land for our power to change it,
To confess our misdoings, to mend what we can,
To learn what we mean and make it the law,
To become what we said we were going to be.

But even such critical patriotism, rightly understood, does not relax for a moment the keen awareness that our true *Patria* is not yet. For those whose primary allegiance is to the City of God, every foreign country is a homeland and every homeland a foreign country. America is our homeland, and, as the prophet Jeremiah says, in its welfare is our welfare. America is also—and history testifies that this is too easily forgotten—a foreign country. Like every political configuration of the earthly city, America, too, is Babylon. It is, for better and worse, the place of our pilgrimage through time toward home. Until the human pilgrimage reaches that destination, which I expect is no time soon, we cannot help but, through our tears, sing the songs of Zion in a foreign land.

II

Meeting God as an American

I ONCE WROTE a book on the American experiment and the idea of covenant. The burden of the book is that a covenantal understanding of America is distinct from, although not incompatible with, a contractual understanding. Most writing about the American experience, and especially about the American political order, takes the "contract theory" of government as a basic premise. Contract theory has a very honorable philosophical pedigree. It is based upon a narrative, some would say a myth, about people entering into a mutually beneficial agreement or contract in order to form a government. The telling of that story by John Locke (d. 1704) had a significant influence on the thinking of the American founders, but it was hardly the only influence, and, in subsequent history has not, I think, been the most important influence.

Time magazine did a long report on my book and highlighted a passage where I had written, "When I meet God, I expect to meet him as an American." Admittedly, that is a statement that can easily be misunderstood. It is certainly not intended as a boast or a claim on God's favorable judgment. It is a simple statement of fact. Among all the things I am or have been or hope to be, I am undeniably an American. (As a matter of biographical fact, I was born in Canada of American citizens, so I have dual citizenship. But I have since childhood elected to be an American.) It is not the most important thing, being an American, but it is an inescapable thing about the life I live.

Identity has become something of a buzz word in our public discussions, leading to the frequently deplored "identity politics" that constructs the world around race, gender, sexual orientation, and other contingencies that should not be expected to bear the weight of the world, or even the weight of defining who you are. And yet identity is important. To borrow a motto from the people at American Express, "Don't leave home without it." Once one leaves a secure world of taken-for-granted realities, one is at a loss without an identity. We want to know who we are in relation to who others are, or who they want us to think they are. I am indebted to the sociologist Peter Berger for the phrase "identity kit." We all have one. They are the pieces of biography that people produce in introducing themselves to strangers, in writing a resume for a job, or in privately measuring their successes and failures. For these purposes and others, any identity is better than none.

One's identity is, as often as not, a work in progress. And it is not entirely a matter of choice. One cannot make it up out of whole cloth. After all, one is born at a particular time and place, with particular parents and other circumstances that shape one's opportunities and expectations. Being an American is among the more important of those circumstances. Needless to say, our identity, who *we* think we are, is formed in large part by who other people think we are. Recall the line of Robert Burns, "Oh, would that God the gift would gee us / to see ourselves as others see us." We hope for that gift not because others necessarily see us more accurately than we see ourselves, but because how we see ourselves is significantly informed by how we think others see us.

Among American thinkers, and not least among American religious thinkers, one frequently encounters an attempt to escape one's time and place, including one's identity as an American. It is a very American thing to try to do. Such escapes are not necessarily attempted because one dislikes America and is uncomfortable with being identified as an American, although that is no doubt sometimes the case. Rather, there is something in American culture, reinforced by frequently unacknowledged Christian impulses, that prompts people to think that they should be *more than* Americans.

An academic friend who teaches religious ethics at a prestigious university fervently insists that she is not an American citizen but "a citizen of the world." You perhaps have friends like that. This is also a very American thing, thinking that we have transcended being American. We are, after all, as some like to say, the world's first "universal nation." By that is meant that we are a "nation of immigrants," and therefore that American identity is an amalgam of the identities of all the peoples of the world. The phrase *universal nation* is also intended to mean that American identity is established not by sharing national origin, ethnicity, race, religion, or other historically contingent features but by subscribing to certain *universal principles*—for instance, the principles set forth in the Declaration of Independence.

Lutheran theologian Robert Jenson employs to fine effect the phrase "the story of the world." The story of the people of Israel and the Church, he writes, is nothing less than the story of the world, and the world is today lost in its confusions because it has "lost its story." I would add that, for those of us who are Americans, we are *as Americans* part of the story that is the story of the world. Moreover, America itself—this nation that the founders called an experiment, and that, like any experiment, may succeed or fail—is part of the story that is the story of the world. Of the many ways of thinking about America—economic, political, cultural, and so on—there is today a striking scarcity of thinking about America religiously, even, if you will, theologically. It was not always so.

This subject touches, of course, on the familiar question of the one and the many, of particularity and universality, and whether, as modernity has led many to think, one must choose between them. The last book published by Pope John Paul II, whom history will, I believe, call John Paul the Great, is entitled *Memory and Identity;* it is a profound reflection on the connections between personhood and peoplehood, between national experience and God's purposes through time, and one's own little place in that drama. Of course, the book is about Poland and being Polish, both of which John Paul explores and affirms in a way that many might think scandalously chauvinistic, but I believe the book is provocatively wise.

It was not so long ago that American intellectuals, including American theologians, thought in a similar way, albeit not always so profoundly, about the American experiment. In the past half century or so, Americans have largely lost their story and its place in the story of the world. Religious thinkers, too, have succumbed to the false-consciousness of having transcended the American experience, which is expressed, more often than not, in a typically American anti-Americanism that is relished and imitated by others, perhaps most notably European intellectuals.

There are many and complex reasons why Americans may feel alienated from their country. John Paul may be excused for perceiving such a close connection between Poland and God's purposes in history. After all, Poland is Poland, a country of middling influence whose very existence its neighbors, mainly Germany and Russia, have for centuries done their best to deny. It is very different with America: the preeminent superpower with its overweening and imperious, if not imperial, force behind the globalization of a meretricious culture in the service of feeding the insatiable appetite of capitalist expansion. At least so America is seen by many in the world, and many Americans have all too keen a gift of seeing themselves as others see them. As in the writing of biography, or of history more generally, one cannot think truly about a story with which one is not sympathetically engaged. And it must be admitted that many Americans are not sympathetically engaged with the story of their country. Love is sometimes blind, but contempt is always blind.

Thought that is real and not merely, as Cardinal John Henry Newman put it, "notional," is thought sympathetically engaged with time and place. The Letter to the

Hebrews reminds us that Christians have here no abiding city. In the third eucharistic prayer of the Catholic Mass there is the prayer, "Strengthen in faith and love your pilgrim Church on earth." Christians are a pilgrim people, a people on the way, exiles from our true home, aliens in a strange land. And yet this strange land is very much our land, even if only for the duration of our exile, which is likely to be long.

There is, as I mentioned earlier, in all the Christian tradition no more compelling depiction of our circumstance than Saint Augustine's *City of God.* Short of the final coming of the Kingdom, the City of God and the earthly city are intermingled. We are to make use of, pray for, and do our share for the earthly city. Here Augustine also cites the words of Jeremiah urging the people not to fear exile in Babylon: "Seek the welfare of the city where I have sent you into exile, and pray to the LORD on its behalf, for in its peace you will find your peace." As we saw in the first chapter, this is a continuing theme in the way Christians think about their place in history.

It is often forgotten how very much of a Roman Augustine was. The *City of God* is, among other things, a sustained argument with pagan interlocutors whom we might today call "public intellectuals"; he is contending for the superiority of the Christian philosophy and understanding of history. One modern scholar has described Augustine as a "culture warrior" in a circumstance not entirely unlike what are called the culture wars of our time. It is sometimes suggested that Augustine knew he was writing in the ruins of a collapsing empire that he dismissed as terminally corrupt. In fact, he wrote, "The Roman Empire has been shaken rather than transformed, and that happened to it at other periods, before the preaching of Christ's name, and it recovered. There is no need to despair of its recovery at this present time. Who knows what is God's will in this matter?" Knowing that we do not know God's will does not mean that we do not think about God's will in this and all matters, for, as Augustine writes in the same text, "It is beyond anything incredible that God should have willed the kingdoms of men, their dominations and their servitudes, to be outside the range of the laws of his providence."

Christians have, at least until fairly recently, tried to understand the part of the American experiment within what Augustine calls the laws of God's providence. In this they followed the precedent of the Great Tradition of Christian thought in other times and places. In the early fourth century, Christianity was made legal under the emperor Constantine, and later it became the established religion. As we have seen, Eusebius saw this as the providentially guided triumph of the gospel. Today, especially but not exclusively among Protestant scholars, the conversion of Constantine and the establishment of what would come to be called "Christendom" is more often viewed as the fall of the Church from its primitive purity.

As the Anglican Oliver O'Donovan reminds us, "Constantinianism," far from being a term of opprobrium, represents a considerable Christian achievement of that place and time. The distinguished church historian Robert Louis Wilken convincingly argues that the toleration and later establishment of the Church was not a corruption in which, as it is sometimes said today, the Church ended up "doing ethics for Caesar." When, in the year 390, Saint Ambrose excommunicated the

Christian Theodosius for his massacre in Thessalonika, he was holding Caesar accountable to the ethics of the Church. Similarly, what is often dismissively referred to as medieval "Christendom" can be seen as a creative coordination, for its time and place, of the tensions between, and the mutual interests of, the earthly city and the City of God. It is within this long and complicated history that one thinks also of the American experiment.

A. D. Lindsay, the British author of the classic work *The Modern Democratic State*, puts the matter nicely:

> The adjustment of the relation between these two societies was, of course, no easy matter. The history of the relations between church and state in the Middle Ages is a history of a long dispute waged with wavering fortune on either side. Extravagant claims made by one side called forth equally extravagant claims on the other. The Erastianism of post-Reformation settlements was the answer to earlier imperiousness on the other side. But the disputes between the secular power and the papacy, however long and embittered, were boundary disputes. Neither party denied that there were two spheres, one appropriate to the church, the other to the state. Even those partisans who made high claims for their side did not deny that the other side had a sphere of its own. They only put its place lower than did their opponents. The Christian always knew that he had two loyalties: that if he was to remember the Apostle's command "to be subject unto the higher powers," he was also to remember that his duty was "to obey God rather than man." There are things which are Caesar's and things which are God's. Men might dispute as to which

> were whose, but the fact of the distinction no one denied.

The Erastianism of which this author speaks is a doctrine named after a sixteenth-century Swiss theologian, Thomas Erastus, who argued for the state's control of spiritual and ecclesiastical matters. The idea was dramatically implemented by Henry VIII, who declared that he, and not the pope, was supreme head of the Church in England. The supremacy of the secular power was very influentially defended by Richard Hooker in his treatise of 1594, *Ecclesiastical Polity.* The political theory and practice of the Western world is the story of a growing Erastianism in which the modern state, brooking no competition from other claims to sovereignty, has attempted to eliminate the "boundary disputes" between temporal and spiritual authorities. The United States in its founding, as is evident in the Religion Clause of the First Amendment, is the great exception to this general pattern. But as we shall see, "American exceptionalism," also on this score, needs constantly to be reexamined and, when necessary, vigorously defended.

We can view the distinctive ways in which American Christians have tried to understand the American story in the light of this long and complex tradition of contesting authorities. These ways have produced at times, with very mixed results, what is aptly termed a "theology of the American experience." The seventeenth-century Puritan settlers understood themselves to be, in historian Perry Miller's happy trope, on an "errand into the wilderness." The image was that of God's chosen people on their way to the promised land. In that way of telling the story, they were the New Israel.

In some tellings of the story, they and the New World *were* Jerusalem, having escaped the captivity of the Babylon of the Old World and, most particularly, having escaped the Babylon of Catholicism and of the insufficiently Protestantized lowercase catholicism that was Anglicanism in the old country. From these Puritan beginnings, American thinking about America would radically reverse the image of exile. In the Puritan view, the Church of *The Letter to Diognetus* and of Augustine, namely Catholicism, is now Babylon, and the foreign country, namely America, is now the Christian homeland. America is Jerusalem. And, in the more fantastical flights of theological imagination, America is something very close to the New Jerusalem.

The eighteenth-century thinker Jonathan Edwards was a leading light of the astonishing spiritual revival called the "First Great Awakening," and he is still today recognized as one of the great theological minds in our national experience. Robert Jenson calls him, quite simply, *America's Theologian,* and many would agree. The evangelical Christianity that figures so prominently in American public life today is not, as many would have it, a phenomenon that appeared with the rise of Billy Graham or the election of Jimmy Carter as president. The emphasis on "experimental religion"—meaning the experience of conversion and revival—goes back to the great awakenings of the eighteenth century and is movingly described in accounts such as Edwards's 1737 report, *A Faithful Narrative of the Surprizing Work of God.*

Edwards and others of like mind believed that with the defeat of "popery," which they identified with the Antichrist, and the outpouring of the Spirit evident in revivals, the End Time could be near. "Tis not unlikely," wrote Edwards, "that this work of God's Spirit is the dawning, or at least a prelude, of that glorious work of God so often foretold in Scripture. . . . There are many things that make it probable that this work will begin in America." (One notes in passing that a distinctively American religion—although in this case an undoubtedly Christian form of religion—did not await Joseph Smith's discovery of the golden tablets in upstate New York.) Other accounts written at the time by people less reflective than Edwards were less conditional in their confidence that God had elected America to play the decisive role in the cosmic story of salvation.

After his visit to this country in the early 1930s, G. K. Chesterton famously remarked that "America is a nation with the soul of a church." The remark is both famous and true. More than that, in the absence of an ecclesiology that tethered them to the Church from its beginnings through every period of its history, for many American Protestant thinkers America became their Church. That was true then, and it is true now. More than 300 years after the First Great Awakening, in yet another reversal that they describe as radical, some theologians today depict America not as the Church or as the precursor of the New Jerusalem, but as Babylon. Of course, America is that, in the sense that everyplace is a place of exile for those whose true home is the City of God. But that is not what these radical critics have in mind.

Whether America is depicted as the anticipation of the New Jerusalem or its antithesis, as the precursor or the enemy of the hoped-for destination, what such thinkers have in common is the lack of a clear connection to the Church in continuity with the Christian story through time. It is not enough for America to have the *soul* of a church. It is an American Protestant trait to forget that, in the biblical image, the Church is not the soul of Christ but the *body* of Christ. It is a distinctive society through time—a society distinct from the societies in which, sometimes for better and sometimes for worse, she is compelled to live through time toward the End Time.

With this in mind, we can better understand the argument of the literary and cultural critic Harold Bloom that "the American religion" is gnosticism. By *gnosticism* is meant the belief—sometimes more implied than explicitly stated—that the particularities of matter, time, and place are merely incidental, if not actually evil. Emancipation is to be found in transcending such particularities by "spiritualities" attuned to esoteric religious knowledge (*gnosis*) or experience. In American evangelicalism, the esoteric—that which is known by the initiated—is to be shared with everyone, thus producing what has been described as the "democratization" of American religion. Since gnostics are the elite, the "knowing ones," democratic gnosticism may seem like a contradiction in terms, but religion in America is notorious for producing improbable combinations of opposites.

Religious gnosticism goes hand in hand with ecclesiological docetism. Docetism was an early Christian heresy which held that Christ only *seemed* to have a human body and to have suffered and died on the cross. Ecclesiological docetism is the idea of an "invisible Church." To be sure, the saints who have gone on to glory are not visible to us, and only God knows who among the living are the truly faithful. But the invisible Church affirmed by many is largely divorced from the Christian story through the centuries and becomes an ethereal and free-floating community separate from the actual community of the Church in time that is, as Newman would say, not notional but real.

These peculiarities have powerfully shaped the American religious sensibility. After the Puritan "errand into the wilderness" came the national founding. With very few exceptions, it was presided over by men who understood themselves to be serious Christians. Even Thomas Jefferson—whom ideological secularists depict as the chief, if not the only, founder—was much more of a Christian than is generally allowed.

In order to advance a principle of freedom, and in order not to threaten the religious establishments of the several states, the founders did a historically unprecedented thing. In the first provision of the First Amendment, they declared that the national government abdicated control of religious belief and practice. To be sure, this was a matter of practical politics as well as principle. Given the competing Protestant denominations of the time, it was unthinkable that the founders would establish one as the national religion. But practical politics can also be in the service of principle.

It would take almost 200 years—the Supreme Court's *Everson v. Board of Education* decision of 1947 is the usual point of reference in this connection—for religious freedom to be radically recast as the government's "neutrality" between religion and irreligion, much to the benefit of irreligion. The consequence is what I have described as the "naked public square." By that phrase is meant the enforced privatization of religion and religiously informed morality, resulting in the exclusion of both from the government of "We the People," we who stubbornly persist in being a vigorously, if confusedly, religious people.

In rebelling against Britain's claim to legitimate authority, the founders appealed to the laws of nature and of nature's God, making the argument that they were acting upon self-evident truths about inalienable rights with which we are endowed by the Creator. The inspiration of the "errand into the wilderness" resonates also in the Great Seal of the United States of America printed on the back of every dollar bill, declaring this America to be a *novus ordo seclorum*—a new order for the ages. Again, the ecclesiological intimations appear; here is a new church, and one hears in the background the voice of the one who promised that the gates of hell shall not prevail against it. Thus was born what some call the American civil religion, a religion that is intricately intertwined with the religion that most Americans call Christianity.

The church of the *novus ordo seclorum* had a thin public theology. In the fine phrase of the political philosopher Leo Strauss, its founding principles were "low but solid." Perhaps too low, and not solid enough. To change the metaphor, the new order was not wired for first-principle questions such as those addressing the humanity and rights of slaves of African descent. As it is not wired for today's questions about the humanity and rights of the unborn child and others who cannot assert their own rights—the questions that are at the vortex of what today are called the culture wars.

In the 1860s the church of the *novus ordo seclorum* was shattered by the bloodiest war in our history, and from that catastrophe emerged the most profound theologian of the civil religion. Lincoln's Second Inaugural Address, with its troubled reflection on the mysteries of providence, is in some ways worthy of Saint Augustine, except, of course, that it is without Augustine's Church, and therefore without the communal bearer of the story of the world by which all other stories, including the story of America, are truly told.

American theology has suffered from an ecclesiological deficit, leading to an ecclesiological substitution of America for the Church through time. Alongside this development, and weaving its way in and out of it, is a radical and vaulting individualism that would transcend the creaturely limits of time, space, tradition, authority, and obedience to received truth. Here the American prince of apostles is Ralph Waldo Emerson, and it is no surprise that he is revered by Harold Bloom as the fount of what he calls the "American Religion." Here there is no doctrine other than what Emerson calls "the doctrine of the soul." The many today who say they are interested in spirituality but not in religion are faithfully following in Emerson's religion and continuing the battle he waged against tradition and the idea of authority. Consider his powerful 1838 address to the divinity students at Harvard:

> Let me admonish you, first of all, to go alone; to refuse the good models, even those which are sacred in the imagination of men, and dare to love God without

> mediator or veil. Friends enough you shall find who will hold up to your emulation Wesleys and Oberlins, Saints and Prophets. Thank God for these good men, but say, "I also am a man." Imitation cannot go above its model. The imitator dooms himself to hopeless mediocrity. The inventor did it, because it was natural to him, and so in him it has a charm. In the imitator, something else is natural, and he bereaves himself of his own beauty, to come short of another man's.

Surveying what he views as the corruptions of historical Christianity with its doctrines, rituals, and traditions of authority, Emerson declares, "The remedy to their deformity is, first, soul, and second, soul, and evermore, soul." Emerson was surely right in saying that "imitation cannot go above its model," and the many who have followed him have, in fact, fallen far short of the Emersonian model. Witness the fate of what used to be called "liberal religion" in the form of Unitarian-Universalism, or visit the shelves upon shelves in the "spirituality" section of your local Barnes and Noble. One can agree with Harold Bloom that gnosticism is the right word for it, if there can be a gnosticism of the masses.

At the same time, there were other American Christians who, remembering the words of Jesus that the servant is not above his master, did not aspire to rise above their model. In the latter part of the nineteenth century, when almost all Protestants called themselves evangelicals, the nation witnessed the impressive construction of the "Benevolent Empire" in what is commonly designated the third great awakening. The Social Gospel movement, led by formidable figures such as Walter Rauschenbusch, embraced the goal of "Christianizing America and Americanizing Christianity." Once again, the note was struck that America is not only a nation with the soul of a church, but is the Church. This self-understanding was soon to be shattered by the fundamentalist-modernist clash of the first part of the twentieth century, giving rise to the conviction that theology, so rife with conflict and divisiveness, must give way to something like a public philosophy.

Here the most notable figure is John Dewey, who died in 1952 at age ninety-two, having presided for six decades as perhaps the most influential public intellectual in American life. Like so many liberal reformers of his time, Dewey was only one step away from the Protestant pulpit. *A Common Faith,* published in 1934, proposed a distinctively American religion that would leave behind the doctrinal and ecclesiological disputes of the hoary past and embrace all people of goodwill in the grand cause of progressive social reform. In what was deemed to be a post-Christian era, here was a new *novus ordo seclorum,* with Americans as the elect people in the vanguard, leading history toward its liberal consummation.

More recently, the late Richard Rorty, the grandson of Rauschenbusch, claimed the mantle of Dewey. The common faith of the elect people lives on. In *Achieving Our Country,* Rorty writes that Dewey and his soulmate Walt Whitman "wanted [their] utopian America to replace God as the unconditional object of desire. They wanted the struggle for social justice to be the country's animating principle, the nation's soul." He quotes favorably the lines of Whitman:

And I say to mankind, Be not curious about God,
For I who am curious about each am not curious about God.

"Whitman and Dewey," Rorty writes, "gave us all the romance, and all the spiritual uplift we Americans need to go about our public business." In this he sets himself against other leftist thinkers whom he accuses of a "semi-conscious anti-Americanism which they carried over from the rage of the late sixties." Their understanding of America's part in the world-historical scheme of things is very different, but Rorty shares with some who call themselves radical Christians a belief that America is front stage center in the cosmic drama. For Rorty, America replaces God as "the unconditional object of desire," while for such Christian radicals America is the Antichrist in pitched battle against God's purposes through time.

Both are quintessentially American in their indifference to Augustine's City of God that is intermingled with the earthly city and on pilgrimage toward the End Time. They are quintessentially American, too, in their indifference to the Church of Augustine that sustains that pilgrimage. (I will be returning to Richard Rorty in a later chapter, for he mirrors so instructively the nature of being American, or at least one way of being American that many thoughtful people find compellingly attractive.)

There are other efforts to establish something like a public philosophy quite apart from overarching claims of providential purpose. To cite an outstanding instance, there was some decades ago John Rawls's *A Theory of Justice.* In this intricately argued work, Rawls proposed that reasonable persons motivated by self-interest and risk-aversion, and unencumbered by a knowledge of their situation in the world, could deliberate behind a "veil of ignorance" and produce an agreement on the principles of a just society.

Rawls, to his great credit, helped revive an interest in political philosophy. Like Aristotle, and against the thinkers for whom politics is all procedure to the exclusion of ends, and especially of moral ends, he understood that politics is the deliberation of how we ought to order our life together. But his "oughtness" was assiduously insulated from what he called "comprehensive accounts" of history and the world. The result was an esoteric theory of slight use in the democratic deliberation of the question, How ought we to order our life together? In his exclusion of accounts of reality that have a popular (that is, democratic) constituency, Rawls is very un-American. From the Puritan beginnings to the founding, from Emerson and Lincoln to Rauschenbusch and Dewey, Americans have been embroiled in what Rawls dismisses as "comprehensive accounts." The perennial effort is to make sense of the story of America within the story of the world.

Among those who have tried to sort through these questions are Reinhold Niebuhr and his brother H. Richard Niebuhr, both of whom were luminaries in the middle of the last century. Reinhold was much better known, but H. Richard's *The Kingdom of God in America* remains instructive reading today. Reinhold was, I believe, much more of a Christian and much more of a Christian thinker than some of his critics, and his fans, will acknowledge. Still today his name is casually invoked by politicians and pundits reaching for a panache of profundity but giving little evidence of having read him.

In many ways Reinhold Niebuhr's sensibility is aptly described as Augustinian. A half century ago and more, both Niebuhrs were in the long tradition of theologians wrestling with the story of America within the story of the world. Reinhold in particular was perhaps too much impressed by what he called "the irony of American history." So skeptical was he of the pridefulness that often accompanied the idea of a national mission—one thinks, for instance, of the notion of America's "manifest destiny" and the dubious purposes to which it was sometimes put—that he failed to constructively engage the irrepressible devotion to a national story, a line of devotion that runs from the "errand into the wilderness" to John F. Kennedy's inaugural declaration: "Let every nation know, whether it wishes us well or ill, that we shall pay any price, bear any burden, meet any hardship, support any friend, oppose any foe, in order to assure the survival and the success of liberty."

Such is the rhetoric of the American story. It is impossible to disassociate the rhetoric from the story. It is not "mere" rhetoric. Rhetoric and story can, of course, be bent to purposes noble or base, wise or foolish. It is the American story, the American promise, that is invoked in Martin Luther King Jr.'s dream of the "beloved community" and in Ronald Reagan's vision of the "city on a hill." Some readers will be surprised and others scandalized by the suggestion that George W. Bush was in the tradition of Washington, Lincoln, Wilson, Kennedy, King, and Reagan in sounding the characteristic notes of the American story, but so it is. Whatever one may think of how those notes were implemented in policy, consider Bush's Second Inaugural Address. Set aside for a moment the popular caricatures of the rough-hewn Texas cowboy and attend to the ringing of the changes in the telling of the national story:

We are led, by events and common sense, to one conclusion: The survival of liberty in our land increasingly depends on the success of liberty in other lands. The best hope for peace in our world is the expansion of freedom in all the world. America's vital interests and our deepest beliefs are now one. From the day of our Founding, we have proclaimed that every man and woman on this earth has rights, and dignity, and matchless value, because they bear the image of the Maker of Heaven and earth. Across the generations we have proclaimed the imperative of self-government, because no one is fit to be a master, and no one deserves to be a slave. Advancing these ideals is the mission that created our Nation. It is the honorable achievement of our fathers. Now it is the urgent requirement of our nation's security, and the calling of our time. So it is the policy of the United States to seek and support the growth of democratic movements and institutions in every nation and culture, with the ultimate goal of ending tyranny in our world. This is not primarily the task of arms, though we will defend ourselves and our friends by force of arms when necessary. . . . The great objective of ending tyranny is the concentrated work of generations. The difficulty of the task is no excuse for avoiding it. America's influence is not unlimited, but fortunately for the oppressed, America's influence is considerable, and we will use it confidently in freedom's cause.

We go forward with complete confidence in the eventual triumph of freedom. Not because history runs on the wheels of inevitability; it is human choices that move events. Not because we consider ourselves a chosen nation; God moves and chooses as He wills. We have

> confidence because freedom is the permanent hope of mankind, the hunger in dark places, the longing of the soul. When our Founders declared a new order of the ages; when soldiers died in wave upon wave for a union based on liberty; when citizens marched in peaceful outrage under the banner "Freedom Now"—they were acting on an ancient hope that is meant to be fulfilled. History has an ebb and flow of justice, but history also has a visible direction, set by liberty and the Author of Liberty.

However ill-advised one may think their policies to be, and however disastrous the results of misguided policies, American presidents typically play a sacerdotal role in situating present purposes within a continuing sacred story. It is a great mistake to dismiss the rhetoric of that story as hypocrisy in the service of ignoble, economic, or imperial ambitions. Both the power and the danger of the story is in the sincerity with which it is told. This was the point so impressively pressed by Reinhold Niebuhr in writing about *The Irony of American History.* Good intentions go awry; we blind ourselves to our own capacity for self-deception when we cast ourselves in the role of God's agents in history's battle between *The Children of Light and the Children of Darkness,* to cite the title of another book by Niebuhr.

It is a "Niebuhrian sensibility" to recognize the wisdom in the concluding observations of his *Irony.* He was writing in 1952 about the contest with the Soviet Union and international communism, but his words are no less pertinent to today's challenge of Islamic Jihadism. Niebuhr wrote:

> There is, in short, even in a conflict with a foe with whom we have little in common the possibility and necessity of living in a dimension of meaning in which the urgencies of the struggle are subordinated to a sense of awe before the vastness of the historical drama in which we are jointly involved; to a sense of modesty about the virtue, wisdom, and power available to us from the resolution of its perplexities; to a sense of contrition about the common human frailties and foibles which lie at the foundation of both the enemy's demonry and our vanities, and to a sense of gratitude for the divine mercies which are promised to those who humble themselves. . . . For if we should perish, the ruthlessness of the foe would be only the secondary cause of the disaster. The primary cause would be that the strength of a giant nation was directed by eyes too blind to see all the hazards of the struggle; and the blindness would be induced not by some accident of nature or history but by hatred and vainglory.

However high our appreciation of America's achievement and promise, and whether that appreciation is expressed from the left, as in the case of Richard Rorty's work, or from the right, as in George W. Bush's speech, with its confidence in a "new order of the ages," the great danger is in forgetting that America, too, is Babylon. Exaggerated patriotism is checked and tempered by the awareness that, while this is a homeland, it is, at the same time, a foreign country. All that having been said, however, it is not just one foreign country among others. There is an irrepressible intuition, from John Winthrop's admonition to the first Puritans on through almost every presidency, that America's story is caught up in the "comprehensive account" of the story of the world.

There was another theologian who was writing at the same time as Reinhold Niebuhr and who has an important place among those who have thought deeply about the American experiment. Father John Courtney Murray, who died in 1967, is best remembered for his part in Dignitatis Humanae, the Second Vatican Council's declaration on religious freedom. But his 1960 book *We Hold These Truths* is an unavoidable point of reference in discussions about America and providential purpose. He had the greatest admiration for the American founders, and admired most of all what he viewed as the modesty of their intention. This constitutional order, he insisted, rested not upon "articles of faith" but upon "articles of peace." Unlike Richard Rorty and many others, America was not his religion. He never confused America with the Church. As a Catholic, he already had a Church that claimed his prior allegiance.

The Church is universal—as in *catholic*—and has centuries of experience with nations and political orders of all varieties, including nations with universal aspirations that compete for that prior allegiance. We see again and again that, without a Church that is not notional but real, without a Church that bears a promise and a purpose that transcend the American experience, the American experience itself, in ways both subtle and vulgar, offers itself as a substitute church.

James Madison wrote in his famed *Memorial and Remonstrance* of 1785 that those who enter the political community must have a prior allegiance to God and the laws of God. That allegiance, said Madison, is prior in both time and importance. For Madison and so many others, however, that allegiance was not embodied and anchored in a community that claimed priority to the political community. Thus, again, America itself became by default a de facto church. Indeed, the fundamental complaint of anti-Catholics in American history is that Catholicism requires a "dual loyalty"—an allegiance to America *and* a prior allegiance to the Church. That was and is exactly right. A prior allegiance is not necessarily a conflicting allegiance. Murray argued that the Catholic allegiance complemented and reinforced the allegiance to the American experiment. In this he agreed with *The Letter to Diognetus* that America is both homeland and foreign country.

Already in 1960, Murray saw that the Protestant establishment, and not least its theological establishment, had wearied of thinking about America in terms of Divine Providence. In *We Hold These Truths,* he anticipated a day when Catholics would have to catch the falling flag of this *novus ordo seclorum.* Murray envisioned a democracy in which citizens were "locked in civil argument" about how we ought to order our life together. He believed that the genius of this American experiment, grounded in what he called the American Proposition, is that it provides the procedures and cultivated habits by which the argument could continue as long as the experiment was sustained. The American Proposition is provisional, not eschatological. The final end, the eschatological end, of history is the promised Kingdom of God. Far short of the Kingdom as we are, that final end is, in present time, anticipated in the life of the Church, especially in the Eucharist of the Church, which is the foretaste of the Feast of the Lamb depicted in the Book of Revelation.

Along the way to the Kingdom, Murray proposed that politics—the deliberation of how we ought to order our life together—is to be guided by natural law. Natural law is by definition not the property of any one religion or denomination, although I believe it has been the providential task of the Catholic Church to guard and to propose again and again the truths of nature and nature's God that were assumed by the American founders.

"From the beginning," wrote Saint Irenaeus in the second century, "God had implanted in the heart of man the precepts of the natural law. Then he reminded him of them by giving the Decalogue." The American founders, without exception, agreed. In Murray's vision, public discourse guided by appeal to natural law—and accompanied by the presence of a Church that effectively challenged democracy's idolatrous aspirations to finality—could provide a public philosophy for sustaining the American experiment in producing as just and free a society as is possible in this our exile from our true homeland.

Talk about a public philosophy for the American experiment strikes many today as nonsensical or utopian. In the view of numerous scholars and philosophers, for example, a common public discourse has been shattered, leaving only the shards of myriad "constructions of reality." Abandoning the very idea of moral truth, politics is no longer the deliberation of how we ought to order our life together but is now, according to some, warfare carried on by other means. All politics is combat politics. There is no longer, we are told, a common American culture, and we should stop pretending that there is. There are only subcultures. Choose your subculture, take up its grievances, contentions, and slogans, and prepare to do battle against the enemy. Liberated from the delusion that opponents in the political arena can together say "We Hold These Truths," we are urged to recognize the futility of being locked in civil argument and accept the fact that there is no substitute for partisan victory.

Such, it is said, is our unhappy circumstance, and many think it not unhappy at all. They relish the battle, with no holds barred, no compromise, and no goal short of the opponents' unconditional surrender. Our circumstance is not entirely new. Today's "culture wars," as they are aptly called, bear striking similarities to the moral and political clashes that existed prior to the Civil War. More than fifty years ago, Walter Lippmann published *The Public Philosophy.* Lippmann in his day was viewed as a national sage of a stature not matched by any public intellectual of our time. In that book, he described a circumstance—before the civil rights movement, before Vietnam, before the cultural and sexual revolutions, before *Roe v. Wade,* before wave upon wave of critical theory and deconstructionisms—not entirely unlike our own. He worried that America was losing its story and was therefore increasingly incapable of engaging in moral discourse and decision. That was a long time ago. And it has been a long time since we have been locked in civil argument premised upon the confidence that we together "Hold These Truths." Lippmann's proposed remedy, to the extent he proposed a remedy, was a recovery of natural law. Although Lippmann was, however ambivalently, a Jew, Reinhold Niebuhr thought the book was altogether too Catholic.

In the half century since Niebuhr, Murray, and Lippmann, the churches that had been a primary bearer of the American story have been of little help in restoring a politics of democratic deliberation about how we ought to order our life together. Those Protestant churches that were once called mainline, and are now viewed as oldline or even sideline, have in recent decades planted the banner "Thus Saith the Lord" on the cultural and political platform of the left. The evangelical Protestant insurgency has planted the same banner on the cultural and political platform of the right. It matters little that those on the right have greater political potency. With notable exceptions, both undermine a religiously informed public philosophy for the American experiment; both contribute to the political corruption of Christian faith and the religious corruption of authentic politics; both have forgotten that, as it is said in the Letter to the Hebrews, we have here no abiding city.

As for the leadership of the Catholic Church in this country, it oscillates between a touching desire to be accepted by the now faded oldline Protestant establishment, on the one hand, and cobelligerency with evangelicalism on great moral and cultural questions, on the other. There are also some Catholics, including bishops and theologians, who remember that the Church is to be the "contrast society" embodying Madison's prior allegiance. As such a contrast society, the Catholic Church is not above the fray, but neither is she captive to the fray. Her chief political contribution is to provide a transcendent horizon for our civil arguments, to temper the passionate confusions of the political penultimate with the theological ultimate, and to insist that our common humanity and gift of reason are capable of deliberating how we ought to order our life together.

And so we return to the beginning. When I meet God, I expect to meet him as an American. Not most importantly as an American, to be sure, but as someone who tried to take seriously, and tried to encourage others to take seriously, the story of America within the story of the world. The argument, in short, is that God is not indifferent toward the American experiment, and therefore we who are called to think about God and his ways through time dare not be indifferent to the American experiment.

America is not uniquely Babylon, but it is our time and place in Babylon. We seek its peace, in which, as Jeremiah said, we find our peace, as we yearn for and anticipate by faith and sacramental grace the New Jerusalem that is our pilgrim goal. It is time to think again—to think deeply, to think religiously—about the story of America within the story of the world. Again, the words of Augustine: "It is beyond anything incredible that God should have willed the kingdoms of men, their dominations and their servitudes, to be outside the range of the laws of his providence."

III

The Idea of Moral Progress

YOU MIGHT SUPPOSE that, during their Babylonian captivity, the only progress, the only promising change, that the people of Israel could look forward to would be a return to their homeland and the rebuilding of the temple in Jerusalem. Yet the word of Jeremiah was that they should for a time remain in Babylon and seek the peace and welfare of that city, in which they would also find their own peace and welfare. The time away from their true home was a time of waiting, but not only of waiting. They were to be engaged in the tasks of that time and place. It could have been otherwise. It could have been a time consumed by bitterness, a place of unrelieved pining for what had been lost.

And so it is that *The Letter to Diognetus* says that Christians take their full part in the tasks of this foreign country that is their homeland. To seek the peace and welfare of Babylon is to seek improvement, and another word for improvement is "progress." Devotion to progress is devotion to the common good, including the good of those citizens of Babylon who seek no other city.

Almost everybody agrees that progress is a good thing. As with most self-evidently good things, however, disagreements arise upon closer examination. And so it is with the idea of progress. Disagreements and confusions multiply when the subject is *moral* progress.

Thinkers arguing from the most diverse perspectives have agreed that few things are so characteristic, indeed constitutive, of modernity as the idea of progress. To be modern is to believe that history is "getting somewhere" in overcoming the problems and limitations of the human condition. It is doubtful that those who call themselves "postmodern" are all that different from the rest of us on this score. And even those who find their excitements in "Apocalypse Now"—often in the form of environmental catastrophe—manage to get out of bed in the morning to join the parade of progress. Although many cannot articulate the reason for the assumption, there is also the implicit belief that getting somewhere means that history is going somewhere. Progress is more than change; it is change with a purpose. Change is the undeniable experience; the idea of progress is a way of understanding the experience.

Change, it is tritely observed, is the only thing that doesn't change. It might almost be said that change is the component of continuity that makes it possible to speak of "history" at all, and to speak of it as one thing. Without *this* happening and then *that* happening—in other words, without change—there would be no history. At the same time, it is said that history is necessarily contingent, which means that what happens is not necessary. Not all of us, but most of us, find it necessary to say that. And those who don't say it live as though it were true. Such are the puzzles entangled in the idea of progress.

We are regularly told that ours is an age of unprecedented rapidity of change. The same was likely said in most every age. One imagines Adam remarking to Eve as they are exiled from the garden, "My dear, we live in an age of rapid transition." The modern assumption is that the transition is to something better. The modern sensibility is frequently that of the neophiliac, the lover of the new. I noticed some while back an advertisement on New York City subways promoting a new computer widget. It bluntly proclaimed the neophiliac creed: "Change is good!" Whether or not there was a philosopher moonlighting at the ad agency, the unarticulated, and perhaps unconscious, assumption is that change is going somewhere; it has an end, it has what the Greeks called a *telos*. As philosophers say, change is *teleological.* Change is good because it is a movement toward the better on history's way toward some unspecified, and perhaps unspecifiable, good. Such is an article of faith in the mindset we call modern.

While more sensible people have problems with the simplistic proposition that change is good, they have equal difficulty with the counterproposition that change is bad. Leaning toward one proposition or the other is thought to mark the difference between dispositions usually called "conservative" and "liberal"—or, as many liberals now prefer, "progressive." Even the most progressive, however, allow that there are setbacks in history, that time is not the vehicle of uninterrupted and smoothly incremental progress. And the most determined conservative, while suspicious of change, will nonetheless allow that there are instances of undoubted progress. To the question of whether there is progress in history, a conservative friend of mine, a distinguished social scientist, responded with the observation that, up until about a hundred years ago, most people went through at least half of their lives with a toothache. In our society today, few people born after 1960 know what a toothache is. QED.

When we think of progress, we likely think most immediately of science, and of medicine in particular. In the early seventeenth century, Francis Bacon championed the conquest of nature through science and technology in order, as he said, to "relieve the human estate." In important ways, the human estate has been relieved. There can be no question about that, and the relief goes far beyond the absence of toothaches. There is undoubted progress also in economic well-being. It is no little thing that in America today those who are officially counted as living in "poverty" have, with relatively few exceptions, a standard of living that was considered "middle class" only fifty years ago. Moreover, there is hardly a product that we buy—from cars to razor blades to bed mattresses—that, controlling for inflation, is not cheaper and better today than twenty-five years ago. Not to mention the many things that were not available then, such as numerous products connected with the digital revolution.

I was in Cuba a few years ago and, walking down one of the decaying streets of Havana, I tried to place a puzzling sound that I heard—a persistent clickity-clack noise coming from what appeared to be a government office. (Almost all offices in Cuba are government offices.) I knew I had heard a sound like that somewhere in what seemed a distant past. Turning a corner, I came upon the source of the sound, a young man sitting in a dark and cavernous room with a single lightbulb. He was filling out forms with triple carbon copies on a manual typewriter. Clickety-clack, clickety-clack. It was a small but telling instance of what, in more developed countries, progress has left behind.

Nor need we content ourselves with technological, medical, and economic evidence of historical advance. Is there not also a phenomenon that is rightly called "moral progress"? Most of us are inclined to answer in the affirmative. In the history of our own country, we have put slavery and legally imposed racial segregation behind us, and almost nobody doubts that this counts as moral progress. More ambiguously, there are the recent decades of changing sex roles and redefinitions of the family. Such changes are, to put it mildly, still controversial, but their proponents express confidence that their recognition as progress is only a matter of time.

Also in the realm of what we might call "political morality," it would seem that we have learned something from the catastrophes of the past. Apart from occasional reports about the weekend militias of white supremacists, nobody today advocates a regime based upon the superiority of Aryan blood. Outside the more rarefied departments of some universities, very few propose socialism in the form of state collectivization of private property. Moreover, it is surely great progress that, at least in the West, we do not kill one another in wars of religion. Whether this is because of a decline in religious commitment or because, as I think more likely, we have come to recognize that it is the will of God that we not kill one another over our disagreements about the will of God, it is undoubtedly a very good thing.

So it is that those who adhere to the gospel of progress are not without considerable evidence to support their faith. Yet there is much evidence that faith in progress is not so robust as it once was. Apart from corporate advertisers declaring that "change is good," full-throated boosterism of the gospel of progress is rare today, although it is true that skilled politicians can, in times of malaise, use the vacuous promise of "change" to rally fevered support for their cause. More thoughtful people, however, have cultivated an informed skepticism about such sloganeering. Perhaps the most quoted poem of our time is W. B. Yeats's 1921 "The Second Coming," in which he observes that "Things fall apart; the center cannot hold." The real or imagined prospect of impending ecological collapse and the all-too-real proliferation of nuclear and other weapons of mass destruction, among other things, cast a pall over the future, suggesting that, to paraphrase another poet, T. S. Eliot, the world may end with both a bang *and* a whimper.

The casting of the pall, in one telling of the story, goes back to the guns of August 1914, when it was said that the lights were going out all over the world. As a college student reading the memoirs of British philosopher Bertrand Russell I recall being deeply impressed by his claim that nobody who was not a child before 1914 could know what real happiness is. In the privileged and enlightened world in which Lord Russell grew up, all good things then seemed possible, indeed almost inevitable. It was only a matter of time. Of the French Revolution, more than a century earlier than Russell, William Wordsworth could exclaim, "Bliss was it in that dawn to be alive, / But to be young was very heaven!" Humanity seems much older now.

To be sure, in recent decades we witnessed a counterculture that, in a spasm of historical amnesia, had flower children announcing the Age of Aquarius to the tune of Bob Dylan's "The Times They Are a-Changin'." The grownups knew better, even if many of them felt obliged to indulge the youthful trashing of the world they had made, a world their children held in contempt. Yet those same children, now beyond middle age and in charge of almost everything, if they are not already drawing Social Security, seem not to believe that the doctrine of historical progress has been vindicated. The Woodstock Nation, named after the Woodstock festival of 1969, was a youthful high, but it is today nostalgically remembered as a "time-out" from the real world, a kind of holiday from history.

How can one seriously believe in progress at the end of what is undeniably the bloodiest hundred years in history—the century of the Battle of the Somme, of obliteration bombing, of Auschwitz, of the Gulag Archipelago, of Chairman Mao's cultural revolution, and of mass starvation as state policy? In this period, so many people have been deliberately killed by other people that the estimates of historians vary by the tens of millions, and the historians end up by agreeing to split the difference or round off the victim count at the nearest 10 million. The estimates of the number of victims of communism alone range from 80 million to 120 million, so for journalistic purposes we settle on 100 million. One might conclude that it has not been a good hundred years for the idea of progress in general, and of moral progress in particular.

Shortly after World War I put out the lights all over the world, Oswald Spengler published his two-volume *Der Untergang des Abendlandes,* known in English as *The Decline of the West.* Professional historians pilloried his scholarship, but many of the brightest and best of a generation suspected he was telling the truth, as they also succumbed to the mood of Eliot's "The Wasteland," published in the same year as Spengler's second volume. A great depression and another world war later, after Henry Luce's "American Century" had been proclaimed and then debunked by Vietnam and all that, Harvard's Robert Nisbet published, in 1980, his *History of the Idea of Progress.* Nisbet believed that, despite spasmodic eruptions of an ever more desperate optimism, the idea of progress was moribund or dead.

The idea of progress, Nisbet wrote, began with classical Greece and its fascination with knowledge, a fascination that was appropriated and put to intellectual and practical use by Christianity. From the early church fathers through the high Middle Ages and into the Puritan seventeenth century of Isaac Newton and Robert Boyle, there was a confidence that ever-expanding knowledge held the promise of something like a golden age. Although often in secular form, this confidence drove an Enlightenment that was living off the capital of Christian faith in historical purpose.

The first words of the Gospel of John are, "In the beginning was the Word." The Word, the *logos,* is the meaning and reason that pervades reality. This is the foundation of the assumed link between knowledge and progress. It is, says Nisbet, the background assumption of the liberal belief in "education" as the panacea for human problems, paving the way toward something like utopia. But by the 1970s, Nisbet adds, thoughtful people were beginning to talk about the limits of knowledge, the end of scientific inquiry, the unreliability of claims to objective truth. The curtain was falling on the long-running show of modernity and progress. What would come to be called "postmodernity" was waiting in the wings.

For many centuries, the argument was that knowledge equals progress, and that now—or at least many were saying—advances in real knowledge were coming to an end. In 1978 an entire issue of the scholarly journal *Daedalus* was devoted to articles by scientists on "The Limits of Scientific Inquiry." Not only did science no longer have the cultural and moral authority that it once enjoyed, but many scientists were filled with doubts about their own enterprise. Some went so far as to suggest that we were perhaps witnessing a reversal of roles between science and religion, with the ascendancy of the latter in providing a more adequate description of our historical circumstance.

A few years earlier, the distinguished molecular biologist Gunther Stent published a widely read little book, *The Coming of the Golden Age: A View of the End of Progress.* There was irony in his reference to a "golden age," for what he discerned was a decline or *stasis* in almost every aspect of scientific, social, and artistic life. His critique was much more subtle than just another lament about growing license and decadence. For instance, he noted that the progress of art in modernity had been accompanied by a freedom from accepted canons and limits, and that this freedom was undoing art itself. "However," Stent wrote, "the artist's accession to near-total freedom of expression now presents very great cognitive difficulties for the appreciation of his work: The absence of recognizable canons reduces his act of creation to near-randomness for the perceiver. In other words, artistic evolution along the one-way street to freedom embodies an element of self-limitation." Can freedom be formless? Or is freedom—of necessity, we might say—either liberation from or aspiration toward form?

Stent noted that a similar sense of limits, of an end of progress, was evident in the so-called hard sciences, including his own field of molecular biology. We may view such claims with a certain skepticism. When the Sumerians invented the wheel, there were perhaps those who observed that this was the end of progress. A French historian wrote in 1687: "Our age is . . . arrived at the very summit of perfection. And since for some years the rate of progress has been much slower and appears almost insensible—as the days seem to cease lengthening when the summer solstice draws near—it is pleasant to think that there are probably not many things for which we need envy future generations." History's destination had been reached, he concluded, or was close at hand.

Gunther Stent, however, did not speak from such smug complacency but from a keen appreciation of scientific facts. He traced the various stages of the ascendancy of scientific progress in understanding ever more complex phenomena. We had now, he said, arrived at "the end of progress" because we had come up against the "mind-matter paradox." Stent asked, "Is it in fact likely that consciousness, the unique attribute of the brain, that appears to endow its ensemble of atoms with self-awareness, will ever be explained?" He answered his own question in the negative, suggesting that the search for a "molecular" explanation of consciousness was "a waste of time." "Thus, as far as consciousness is concerned, it is possible that the quest for its physical nature is bringing us to the limits of human understanding, in that the brain may not be capable, in the last analysis, of providing [an] explanation of itself."

Today, the connection between brain, mind, and consciousness is the subject of heated debate among scientists, philosophers, and theologians. One elementary problem may be put this way: The human brain would have to be a great deal more simple than it is in order for us to understand it; but if the brain were simple enough for us to understand it, our brains would be too simple to understand it. It is something of a quandary, and that quandary hardly begins to touch on the deeper questions about the relationship between brain, mind, and consciousness.

Yes, there are those who embrace simple-minded responses to the quandary. In recent years, the "new atheists," as they are misleadingly called, such as Richard Dawkins, say that we human beings are nothing but "survival machines" and that what we call thought is nothing more than the product of neurosynapses in the pound of meat that is the brain. But, by their own account, they are programmed to talk that way, and, apart from our sympathy for their self-chosen plight, we need pay no mind to what they insist on describing as their mindlessness. Of course they protest that they are making an argument that has a claim upon our intellectual attention, but, try as we might, we cannot agree without denying the existence of the intellect that is the agent of our agreement.

There are other ways in which the limits of science come to the fore. To cite but one obvious instance, cosmologists who study the structure of space-time relationships in the universe note that the billions of light-years between ourselves and the reception of the data that we can examine means that we never know what is happening *now* billions of light-years away (or even what "now" means in this context). And the very logic of the circumstance means that it will not, it cannot, change in the future. Scientists a billion years from now, if we can imagine such a thing, will still be billions of light-years away from the data accessible to their scrutiny. Even if, in ways that are not now imagined, we were able to leapfrog, so to speak, over vast spaces of time, there would always be—beyond any point reached—an infinity of points not reached. In other words, there is no end, and it is that realization that is at the heart of the idea of the end of progress.

Those of us who are not astronomers, physicists, or molecular biologists cannot help but follow these discussions with great interest. Of most particular interest to the theologian and philosopher is the discussion of the mind-matter connection, which, especially in light of what physicists call the "anthropic principle," is richly suggestive for the biblical understanding of humanity created in the image and likeness of God—human beings as participants, if you will, in the mind of God. Scientific thought moves in antithetical directions. On the one hand, it would reduce reason and consciousness to nothing more than matter in motion; on the other, it explores the anthropic prejudice built into reality by which man participates in the *logos* of all that is. But exploring these questions in greater detail here would take us too far afield.

The question at hand is the idea of progress, and how that idea is now challenged not only by events in politics, society, and culture, but also by science, which, following its own rigorous methodology, discovers that there are many things we do not know and can never know. One may object that these limits are at the margins, that there are still vast fields of discovery open to future generations, which is true. But that is the way it is with limits; they are, by definition, always at the margin. They define the margins.

The crucial point is that the link between knowledge and progress that was forged in classical Greece and that, in the form we call scientific, has been both the motor and the guarantor of the modernity project has now been broken. Or so we are told by some of the more impressive thinkers of our time. The somewhat Spenglerian telling of the cultural story is summed up in the massive book published in 2000 by historian and critic Jacques Barzun, *From Dawn to Decadence: 1500 to the Present; 500 Years of Western Cultural Life.* As his title suggests, he provides naught for our comfort. Having lived through so much change that turned out bad,

Barzun, like others of a certain age, harbors a strong measure of skepticism about the slogan "Change is good."

In the epilogue to his rather melancholy book on the subject, Robert Nisbet asks the question, "What is the future of the idea of progress in the West?" He continues: "Any answer to that question requires an answer to a prior question: what is the future of Judeo-Christianity in the West?" He notes that the great thinkers of the Enlightenment—for instance, Gotthold Ephraim Lessing, Immanuel Kant, Johann Gottfried von Herder, and Joseph Priestley—all recognized that the idea of progress was "closely and deeply united with Christianity." The same is true of the enormously influential prophets of progress. Nisbet notes: "The mature writings of Saint-Simon and Comte, both preeminent in the history of the idea of progress, bear this out. Even Mill, apparent atheist through much of his life, came in his final years to declare the indispensability of Christianity to both progress and order." As for Karl Marx, it is by now a commonplace to observe that his grand ideological structure of the dialectic of history was a heretical—and, as put into practice, massively lethal—variation on Christian themes.

Although Nisbet's melancholy goes deep, he expresses the hope, perhaps a wan hope, that something like a religious awakening might yet rescuc thc idea of progress. He saw signs of such an awakening, and in succeeding years many have thought those signs grew stronger. Nisbet quotes Yeats: "Surely some revelation is at hand?" Maybe. Maybe not. Nisbet concludes his book with this: "Only, it seems evident from the historical record, in the context of a true culture in which the core is a deep and wide sense of the *sacred,* are we likely to regain the vital conditions of progress itself and of faith in progress—past, present, and future."

Progress as dogma. Progress as faith. It sounds very much like a religion—the Religion of Progress. That progress has become a false religion, indeed an idol, has been the worry of many Christian thinkers in the modern era. Few have expressed that concern with such incisiveness and prophetic passion as Reinhold Niebuhr. No American theologian since Niebuhr, who died in 1971, has had such a wide influence in our intellectual culture. A champion of what was called "neo-orthodoxy," Niebuhr attacked precisely the link between Judeo-Christian religion and the idea of progress that Robert Nisbet and many others have wanted to revive. In a 1939 lecture Niebuhr noted: "The idea of progress is possible only upon the ground of a Christian culture. It is a secularized version of Biblical apocalypse and of the Hebraic sense of a meaningful history, in contrast to the meaningless history of the Greeks."

Niebuhr did not intend that as a compliment to Christian culture. His point is that the idea of progress is a cultural distortion of authentic Christianity. A staunch Protestant writing in an era before the full flowering of ecumenical etiquette, Niebuhr blamed this distortion on what he called the "Catholic synthesis" of nature and grace as that synthesis was secularized in the Renaissance and, subsequently, in modernity. The secularized idea of progress emerged from the biblical understanding of purpose in history, said Niebuhr, but it broke away from the biblical truth that the fulfillment of history transcends history itself, as it also jettisoned any notion of Divine judgment. The secularized story of history therefore ended up with "no consciousness of the ambiguous and tragic elements in history." It is true, said Niebuhr, that human history is filled with endless possibilities, but the false gospel of progress forgets that they are endless possibilities for both good and evil. "History, therefore, has no solution of its own problem."

Niebuhr was accused of offering a bleak or pessimistic view of history. He called it "Christian realism." As an Augustinian of the realist school, he stressed the limits of history and therefore the need to rely on hope. John Rawls was an Augustinian of the procedural sort, determined to make do within the limits of history, and his passion was for the virtue of justice. The Catholic Augustinians whom Niebuhr criticized so sharply were of the school of the *logos,* where it is understood that reason participates in the Mind of the Maker, and all that is truly real is love in response to the love by which all that is exists. Love takes the form of justice within the limits of history and is vivified by hope that such limits are not forever.

If, without the idea of progress, people might despair of the tasks of personal, social, and scientific advance, that, too, said Niebuhr, might be to the good. There is such a thing as "creative despair" that induces faith, he said, and such faith "becomes the wisdom which makes 'sense' out of a life and history which would otherwise remain senseless." What we should have learned from the past 200 years, and especially from the catastrophes of the twentieth century, is that history is not the answer to the question that is history. Niebuhr puts the point nicely: "We have learned, in other words, that history is not its own redeemer." It is a pity that Niebuhr did not recognize that Catholic Augustinians did not disagree. Or, to put it differently, the Catholic "synthesis" is that the Creator and Redeemer has entered history through the incarnation of the *logos* in Jesus the son of Mary; the transcendent and the immanent, the infinite and finite, are so conjoined that history, while it is not its own redeemer, does participate in its own redemption.

One may be unpersuaded by some of Niebuhr's conclusions, but a Niebuhrian sensibility is an invaluable safeguard against the shallow sentimentalisms and utopian fantasies that have all too often afflicted thinking about history and its possibilities. Niebuhr rightly reminds us that history is not the uninterrupted triumphal march of progress. In the Christian view of things, experience both personal and social is cruciform; it is the way of the cross. At the same time, the cross is not the final word. There is resurrection, and it is both resurrection *in* history and resurrection *of* history. It is first the resurrection of the history of Jesus, which is the promise and foretaste of the resurrection of all things.

That is the significance of Saint Paul's great cosmic hymns in, for instance, the first chapters of Ephesians and Colossians. To the Ephesians Paul writes, "For [God] has made known to us in all wisdom and insight the mystery of his will, according to his purpose which he set forth in Christ as a plan for the fullness of time, to unite all things in him, things in heaven and things on earth." Babylon is not forever.

This vision is inseparable from an emphatically Jewish understanding of the Messianic Age. The chief difference between Jews and Christians is over if, or in what way, that Messianic Age is anticipated in the person of Jesus whom Christians call the Christ. For both Christians and Jews, past and present time participate in what Paul calls "the fullness of time." In the call of Abraham, the election of Israel, the promises given through the prophets, and (for Christians) the coming of the Christ, the plan of history is being fulfilled. Jews disagree with Jews—and Christians disagree with Christians—over the eschatological scenarios and apocalyptic details by which "the fullness of time" will be achieved, but all are agreed that history is not, in the words of the cynic, just one damned thing after another. History will realize its *telos* in the Kingdom of God. Niebuhr is undoubtedly right to say that "history is not its own redeemer." But the biblical view—a view that is utterly formative for Western culture in both its religious and secular expressions—is that history does have a Redeemer, and that Redeemer is, however veiled and sometimes hidden, present and active in history.

Niebuhr's relentlessly Protestant reading of history is, as he recognized, in tension, if not in conflict, with the "Catholic synthesis." In our own time, that synthesis was energetically set forth by Pope John Paul the Great. In his 1998 encyclical *Fides et Ratio* (Faith and Reason), he makes the argument that there can be no conflict between faith and reason, between science and religion, between philosophy and revelation. All truth is one because God, the source and end of all truth, is one. Human beings are by nature seekers after truth, and revelation provides the ultimate "horizon" of that search. The Word of God, or the *logos* that is the ordering reason of all things, is incarnate in history and is the guarantee that the search for truth is not in vain. Not until the final End Time will we know the truth in full, but along the way both believers and unbelievers who honestly seek for the truth according to the rules of reason will be vindicated.

This is surely an audacious vision, but is it a doctrine of progress? The answer is yes and no, but we must attend to the no before we can understand the yes. If by progress we mean a smooth, incremental, almost automatic movement in time from worse to better, from ignorance to enlightenment, the answer is certainly no. If, however, by progress we mean that human beings are free agents who are capable of participating in the transcendent purpose that, being immanent in history, holds the certain promise of vindicating all that is true, good, and beautiful, then the answer is certainly yes.

Moral progress, however, is far from being self-evident. We have already noted the events of this century past that have so brutally battered the idea of moral progress. We should at least be open to the possibility that we are today witnessing not moral progress but a dramatic moral regression. While, as we have seen, practitioners in the hard sciences express a new humility about the limits of their knowledge and control, many who work in the field of ethical theory and practice exhibit an extraordinary self-confidence, bordering on and sometimes crossing the line into the vice of hubris.

One thinks, for instance, of Princeton University's Peter Singer. He is not necessarily the most egregious example of such hubris, but he is among the more consistent and candid. Singer is famous, of infamous, for his championing of animal rights as equal or, in some instances, superior to human rights, and for his proposal, among other things, that there should be an extended trial period after the birth of human babies in which those who are defective may be legally killed. Because of his advocacy of infanticide and eugenics, Singer has been denied a platform in German universities, where, after the Hitler era, there is a more vivid memory of such arguments and their consequences.

Singer is no marginal figure in our intellectual culture. In addition to his Princeton professorship, he is author of the main article on the history of ethics, a full twenty pages, in the fifteenth edition of the Encyclopedia Britannica. From Confucius and Aristotle, to Maimonides and Aquinas, through David Hume and Kant to Peter Singer, the article traces the liberation of moral theory and practice from any truths that pose an obstacle to our will to power and control. The gist of it is caught in the title of Singer's 1995 book, *Rethinking Life and Death: The Collapse of Our Traditional Ethics.*

That Singer does not regret the collapse of what he refers to as traditional ethics is evident in the chilling conclusion of his Britannica article: "The culmination of such advances in human reproduction will be the mastery of genetic engineering. . . . Perhaps this will be the most challenging issue for 21st-century ethics." As people of this persuasion frequently put it, we have at last arrived at the point in history in which human rationality and control can take over from what has been the blind evolutionary processes of nature.

Professor Singer leaves no doubt that he welcomes the challenge and the brave new world it portends. The cosmologists and molecular biologists reach the end of knowledge, at which point they fall silent in what might be viewed as a recognition of our human creatureliness. Ethical theorists reach the end of knowledge, at which point anything can be said, and anything can be done. I have elsewhere described Peter Singer as "the philosopher from nowhere." His ethical theory exults in its liberation from particular time and place and from the authoritative references that have shaped our traditions of the moral life.

He calls his approach "preference utilitarianism," in which moral truth—if it still makes sense to speak of moral *truth*—is what we prefer it to be. As I say, Singer is by no means alone among contemporary ethicists, but he is notable for his consistency and candor. He likes to say, for instance, that he and the pope are in complete agreement that the unborn child is, from conception onward, indisputably a human being. The difference is that he, unlike the pope, believes that some human beings, born and unborn, have no right to life that we are morally obliged to respect.

"Preference utilitarianism" is of a piece with a moral disposition that is summed up in the slogan "pro-choice." It is a striking oddity of our time that people who ground morality in choice are frequently the same people who claim that we have no choice. That is to say, they subscribe to the dismal idea that our lives and what we call our thoughts, purposes, and choices are all *determined* by matter in motion—which is, finally, all that we are. At the same time, they subscribe to the idea of progress as the conquest of nature to, as Francis Bacon said, "relieve the estate of man."

In short, we are completely captive to the nature we are determined to conquer. We are free to think and to choose, but our thinking and choosing is an illusion, since in reality they are no more than the transmission of impulses between the neurons of the "pound of meat" that is the brain. As the befuddled philosopher is supposed to have said, "As to the question of whether we have free will, we have no choice but to answer yes." This is self-referential contradiction and intellectual incoherence of a high order. It is at the core of the position that asserts with adamant certitude that there is no truth and that's the truth.

For a dramatically different account of the history of ethics and its progress or regress, there is Alasdair MacIntyre's much-discussed and eminently readable little book *After Virtue*. It is, in my judgment, one of the most important and persuasive books on moral philosophy to be published in the past hundred years. For MacIntyre, the account of moral theory and practice offered by people such as Professor Singer results in a rationalized irrationality in which ethics has broken loose from any tradition of virtue or truth—from our *knowledge* of virtue and truth. The stark choice facing us, MacIntyre says, is a choice between Aristotle or Friedrich Nietzsche—between a tradition of reason and virtue, on the one hand, and moral nihilism, on the other. Many of the intellectual dispositions that today run under the banner of "postmodernism" have quite consciously opted for nihilism. The hubris of Enlightenment rationalism that Niebuhr rightly criticized has given way to the hubris of postmodernity's rationalized irrationality.

In the view of MacIntyre and others, the Enlightenment project has failed on its own terms. Despite monumental efforts, perhaps the greatest of which is that of Immanuel Kant, it failed to produce an ethics to which any rational person, acting rationally, must give assent. Society was for a time able to live off the capital of earlier traditions of virtue, but now that capital has been depleted, the failure of the Enlightenment project has been widely advertised, and the time has come round at last for the triumph of nihilism.

In this reading, postmodernity may be viewed either as hyper-modernity or as the product of failed modernity, and the nihilistic avant garde is a regression to the rule of the barbarians. Barbarians today, as in classical Greece, are defined as those who are outside the civilizational circle of conversation about how we ought to order our life together, about the meaning of right and wrong, good and evil. They are those who know nothing and insist that nothing can be known about such matters. Yet they admit that we have no choice but to choose, to act upon our preferences, in the full awareness that we can appeal to no authority beyond our willing it to be so.

In the famous concluding passage of *After Virtue*, MacIntyre draws the parallel between our time and the collapse of the Roman Empire, when Saint Benedict's monastic movement provided a refuge for civilization and a base from which civilization could be rebuilt. MacIntyre writes:

> What matters [now] is the construction of local forms of community within which civility and the intellectual and moral life can be sustained through the new dark ages which are already upon us. And if the tradition of the virtues was able to survive the horrors of the last dark ages, we are not entirely without grounds for hope. This time however the barbarians are not waiting

> beyond the frontiers; they have already been governing us for quite some time. And it is our lack of consciousness of this that constitutes part of our predicament. We are waiting not for a Godot, but for another—doubtless very different—St. Benedict.

We may think this picture somewhat overdrawn. After all, those who are called barbarians are not primitives, and they are not neanderthals; they are frequently those who are academically certified to be the "brightest and best" among us. But that is to miss the point. The new barbarians are not barbarians because they are unsophisticated but precisely because of the hypersophistication with which they have removed themselves from what I have called the civilizational circle of moral conversation. In simpler terms, we may speak of "traditional values." The barbarians refuse to be limited by what we know, by the wisdom we have received, about good and evil, right and wrong.

For them, the past is *merely* prelude. The wisdom of history is disenfranchised. Only the present gets a vote. Nietzsche has triumphed, or so it seems. What the powerful agree to call truth is what we *will* to be. In the beginning is not the Word but the Act. Truth is not discerned or discovered but is the product of our acting, knowing all the while that the action we call "choice" is only an illusion, for all our thinking, choosing, and acting is, in turn, the product of those little synapses in the brain following their predetermined course. And so it is that Nietzsche in his apparent triumph is finally defeated as the will to power is exposed in all its pitiful impotence. One can choose to be a Darwinian or a Nietzschian, but, were they aware of the intellectual incoherence of our time, I am rather sure those two brilliant thinkers would insist on the obviousness of the fact that one cannot be both. We cannot be, at the same time, both the captives and the masters of nature.

What, then, can we say about the future of moral progress? Within the civilizational circle, there is moral progress (and regress!) in how we live, but there is no progress in the sense of moving beyond the moral truths that constitute the circle itself. We can develop the further implications of those truths, or we can step outside the circle by denying that there is such a thing as moral truth. It has become the mark of hyper-sophistication in our time to echo the question of Pontius Pilate, "What is truth?" Pontius Pilate, an urbane Roman governor ever so much more sophisticated by worldly standards than the prisoner who stood before him, was a forerunner of the barbarians who would be—and, according to MacIntyre, already are—our governors today.

Permanent truths are sometimes called natural law. In the Declaration of Independence they are called the laws of nature and nature's God. Or they are called the first principles of ethics. First principles are, by definition, always first. Moral analysis cannot go beyond or behind them any more than human consciousness can go beyond or behind human consciousness. C. S. Lewis, borrowing from Confucianism, called these first principles "the Tao." In *The Abolition of Man,* he anticipated with great prescience today's debates in biomedical ethics about reproductive technologies, genetic engineering, and eugenic progress. The Tao, Lewis said, draws support from all religious and moral traditions in inculcating certain rules, such as general beneficence toward others, special beneficence toward one's own community, duties to parents and ancestors, duties to children and posterity, and the laws of justice, honesty, mercy, and magnanimity. Whether drawn from the Torah, Chinese *Analects,* Cicero, the New Testament, or the *Baghavad Ghita,* these are the truths that constitute the civilizational circle.

Like all tradition, the Tao is vulnerable. Those who want to violate it ask, "Why not?"—and it is not always possible to give a rationally convincing answer, or an answer that is convincing to everybody. In response to the assertion of rules that set limits, the avant garde offers the challenge, "Sez who?" The invoking of authority, even of the most venerable authority, carries little weight with such people. Indeed, if an assertion is supported by authority, that is, in the view of many, a mark against it. Especially if the authority is viewed as being religious in nature.

Most corrosive is what is called the hermeneutics of suspicion, in which every rule, or law, or custom is perceived to have behind it some hidden purpose, some power protecting its own interests. Thus the Tao is debunked, we "see through" its supposed authority, and the force of its commands and limits are "explained away." The result is what Professor Singer approvingly calls "the collapse of traditional ethics." Clearly recognizing what was happening in our intellectual culture, Lewis wrote:

> But you cannot go on "explaining away" for ever: you will find that you have explained explanation itself away.

> You cannot go on "seeing through" things for ever. The whole point of seeing through something is to see something through it. It is good that the window should be transparent, because the street or garden beyond it is opaque. How if you saw through the garden too? It is no use trying to "see through" first principles. If you see through everything, then everything is transparent. But a wholly transparent world is an invisible world. To "see through" all things is the same as not to see.

To which many of our contemporaries say, "Precisely. To see through the first principles of ethics is to see nothing, which means to see that there is nothing except what *we will* to do." So speak the barbarians among us. Whether they rule us to the degree that MacIntyre suggests, I do not know. Whether they will rule us in the future depends upon parents, religious leaders, educators, politicians, artists, writers, and, not least, scientists who understand that there is no progress *beyond* but only *within* the civilizational circle of the truths into which we were born and which we must sustain for those who come after us. And it depends not only on them having this understanding, but on how they give public effect to their understanding.

The moral wisdom of the past must be renewed ever and again by *decision*. This truth is addressed by Pope Benedict XVI in his 2007 encyclical *Spe Salvi* (Saved in Hope):

> We must acknowledge that incremental progress is possible only in the material sphere. Here, in our growing knowledge of the structure of matter and in the light of

> ever more advanced inventions, we clearly see continuous progress toward an ever greater mastery of nature. But in the field of ethical awareness and moral decision-making, there is no similar possibility of accumulation for the simple reason that man's freedom is always new and he must always make his decisions anew. These decisions can never simply be made for us in advance by others—if that were the case, we would no longer be free. Freedom presupposes that in fundamental decisions every person and every generation is a new beginning. New generations can build on the knowledge and experience of those who went before, and they can draw upon the moral treasury of the whole of humanity. But they can also reject it, because it can never be self-evident in the same way as material inventions. The moral treasury of humanity is not readily at hand like tools that we use; it is present as an appeal to freedom and [as evidence of] freedom's possibility.

The people of Israel who were sent into Babylonian exile took with them the law received through Moses. We in our Babylonian exile are the bearers of the moral wisdom of Athens and Jerusalem and of centuries of reflection on the *logos* and the *telos* of reality. Some describe that wisdom in terms of the natural law, meaning by that the moral truths that we cannot *not* know. Others will call it the Tao. Against our fellow Babylonians who seek no other city and have repudiated the truths upon which this earthly city is founded, we follow the counsel of Jeremiah in attempting to secure and advance the peace and welfare that serve the common good, which is the limited and penultimate good that is possible short of the ultimate good that is the New Jerusalem.

Arguments about moral progress and much else of real consequence will not be definitively "won" or "lost" short of that *telos.* It has been said that there are no permanently lost causes because there are no permanently won causes, and the reverse is also true. The young person starting out will, in due course, be the old person ending up, and the success of a life will be measured by whether it was lived in, and courageously contended for, the continuing community claimed by truth beyond our sure possession except by the faith, hope, and love that require nothing less than everything.

IV

Can an Atheist Be a Good Citizen?

THE BABYLONIANS WERE not atheists. Recall all those temples dedicated to sundry gods: Ninmah, Gula, Ninurta, Ishtar, Nabu, and, most prominently, Marduk. We don't have anything like complete information about their specific beliefs and rituals, but it is obvious that, as in all human cultures, there was a lively sense of the interpenetration between human affairs and supernatural powers. The word "culture," we do well to remember, is derived from "cult." Of the sundry cults of a later Roman Empire, Edward Gibbon, a master of the scintillating sneer, said that the vulgar masses thought them equally true, the philosophers thought them equally false, and the rulers thought them equally useful. There no doubt was and is a measure of truth in that—in Babylon of the seventh century B.C., in Rome of the first century A.D., and in America today.

In recent years a slew of books promoting atheism has hit the best-seller lists. They are typically not scholarly inquiries into the existence of God or the complex dynamics of human reflection on the transcendent, but angry broadsides smiting hip and thigh everything associated with religion. Quite predictably, these attacks have elicited in reaction a slew of books attacking the attackers. It is hard to know what to make of this. Atheism at a fever pitch of polemical fury was thought to have gone out of fashion with the stereotype of the "village atheist," who was usually situated in the late nineteenth or early twentieth century. Robert Ingersoll, who died in 1899, was one of the most popular orators of his day, galvanizing crowds by melodramatically taking out his pocket watch and daring God, if there was a God, to strike him dead in the next ten minutes. Audiences waited with bated breath. He lived to do it again at the next stop on the lecture tour, and the next, and the next, until he undramatically succumbed to congestive heart failure at age sixty-five.

The best-selling status of recent books shows that there is in this religion-riddled country still a mass market for the promotion of atheism. Perhaps it is the shock value of the thing that titillates the otherwise devout. Some commentators opine that the popularity of these books reveals the fragility of religious belief and go on to claim that the "new atheism" is the wave of the future. My guess is that these books are a last gasp of angry protest against a world that is becoming ever more overtly religious.

Often with reference to the great sociologist of the early twentieth century, Max Weber, social analysts developed what came to be called "secularization theory." The theory, briefly stated, is that there is a necessary connection between modernization and secularization.

As people become more modern—meaning more educated and technologically competent—the world becomes ever more "disenchanted." God and gods, demons and supranatural powers are banished, having been replaced with "scientific" explanations of an ever more disenchanted world. The contemporary sociologist Peter Berger, a foremost proponent of secularization theory, explained how "the sacred canopy" that once hovered over everyday life and provided ultimate meanings has collapsed under the force of modernity. In more recent years, he has acknowledged that secularization theory was fundamentally flawed. The world is becoming, not less, but more religious.

Not only is there the newly assertive presence of Islam on the world scene, but, as many have pointed out, there are similar religious revivals of Hinduism and Buddhism, as well as the explosive growth of Christianity in what is called the "Global South" of Africa, Asia, and Latin America. The old secularization theory, especially as it was propounded by Western European thinkers, frequently referred to "American exceptionalism." That phrase referred to the puzzling fact (at least it was puzzling to secularization theorists) that the United States, the most modern of societies, stubbornly continued to be so very religious. Today it is more commonly recognized that the cause of puzzlement is "European exceptionalism." The advanced secularization of Europe—meaning especially France, Germany, Spain, and Scandinavia—stands in glaring contrast to the vitality of religion in the rest of the contemporary world.

If the legendary man or woman from Mars was to visit planet earth and ask about the most important thing happening in our world, we might come up with several possible answers. A strong candidate for the best answer would be that the most important single thing happening today is the *desecularization* of world history. If we do not recognize that reality, it is, in large part, because many of us have been overeducated (read indoctrinated) not to recognize it. From grade school through graduate school, textbooks have instilled the idea that, as the world becomes more modern, as people become more educated, as science continues its relentless course, the hold of religion will be weakened, and that, if it does not fade away altogether, it will be banished from public life and consigned to the sphere of private and somewhat eccentric indulgence by people who are interested in that sort of thing.

That understanding is beautifully caught in Matthew Arnold's "Dover Beach" of 1867:

The Sea of Faith
Was once, too, at the full, and round earth's shore
Lay like the folds of a bright girdle furled.
But now I only hear
Its melancholy, long, withdrawing roar,
Retreating, to the breath
Of the night-wind, down the vast edges drear
And naked shingles of the world.

The sense of the melancholy, long, withdrawing roar of the sea of faith is still dominant among many who occupy the commanding heights of our culture. The aforementioned Peter Berger is fond of noting that the most thoroughly secularized country in the world is Sweden, and the most religion-saturated is India. From which he draws the conclusion, "America is a society of Indians ruled by an elite of Swedes." Yes, that goes too far, but it is an exaggeration with an instructive point.

Whether the "new atheism" represented by best-selling books is something new, or simply varieties of old atheism reappearing in a more angry, aggressive, and proselytizing form, is eminently debatable. There is atheism and then there is atheism. The Greek *a-theos* means one who is "without God." In the antiquity of Greece and Rome, it had less to do with whether one believed in God than with whether one publicly reverenced the gods of the city or the empire. For his perceived disbelief in the gods, Socrates was charged with atheism. The early Christians were charged with atheism for their insistence that there was no god other than the God of Israel whom Jesus called Father. In the eyes of the ancients, to be *a-theos* was to be outside the civilizational circle of the *civitas*. To be an atheist was to be a subversive undermining the social order. The atheist was a security risk, if not a traitor. Christians were thought to be atheists precisely because they professed the God who judged and debunked the false gods of the *civitas*. In the classical world, then, the answer to our question was decisively in the negative: No, an atheist could not be a good citizen. But those whom they called atheists then we do not usually call atheists today. Christians, for instance.

Those whom we call atheists in the modern period believe that they are denying what earlier "atheists," such as the Christians, affirmed. That is to say, they deny the reality of what they understand believing Jews and Christians and Muslims to mean by "God." This form of atheism is a post-Enlightenment and largely nineteenth-century phenomenon. It developed a vocabulary that was strongly prejudiced against believers. Note the very use of the term "believer" to describe a person who is persuaded of the reality of God. The alternative to being a believer is to be a "knower." Similarly, a curious usage developed with respect to the categories of faith and reason, the subjective and the objective, and, in the realm of morals, a sharp distinction between fact and value. Belief, faith, subjectivity, values—these were the soft and dubious words relevant to affirming God. Knowledge, reason, objectivity, fact—these were the hard and certain words relevant to denying God.

This tendentious vocabulary of modern unbelief is still very much with us today. Against such tendentious vocabulary, one may argue, as does Michael Polanyi in his classic work *Personal Knowledge,* that everyone who thinks is a believer—the atheist no less than those whom we conventionally call believers. As Polanyi explains, all knowledge is personal in the sense that we have no choice but to make personal decisions about ways of knowing and, consequently, what we believe to be true. There is an inescapable dimension of faith and trust in our knowing, not least of all faith and trust in authority and authorities, such as those who don the mantle of "science." Thus there is no contradiction in our saying, for instance, that we *believe* in science.

The pitting of faith against reason and belief against knowledge undergirds the common assumptions about what is public and what is private. One recalls A. N. Whitehead's maxim that religion is what a man does with his solitude. Even one so "religiously musical" (the phrase is Max Weber's) as William James could write in his great work *The Varieties of Religious Experience,* "Religion . . . shall mean for us the feelings, acts, and experiences of individual men in their solitude." In this way of thinking there is a radical departure from the public nature of religion, whether that religion has to do with the ancient gods of the city or with the biblical Lord who rules the nations. The gods of the city and the God of the Bible are emphatically public. The confinement of the question of God or of the gods to the private sphere constitutes what might be described as political atheism. Many today who are believers in private have been persuaded, or intimidated, into accepting political atheism. This powerfully contributes to what I have elsewhere described as "the naked public square."

Political atheism is a subspecies of practical or methodological atheism. Practical or methodological atheism is, quite simply, the assumption that we can get along with the business of life without addressing the question of God one way or another. Here the classic anecdote is the response of the Marquis de Laplace to Napoleon Bonaparte. When Napoleon observed that Laplace had written a huge book on the system of the universe without mentioning the Author of the universe, Laplace replied, "Sire, I have no need of that hypothesis." When God has become a hypothesis, we have traveled a very long way from both the gods of the ancient city and the God of the Bible. Yet that distance was necessary for the emergence of what the modern world has called "atheism."

The remarkable thing is that the defenders of religion so uncritically accepted the terms of the debate set by the Enlightenment *philosophes* and their later imitators. It is far from evident that the God whom Christians affirm and the god whom atheists deny is the same god. Recall the statement of Blaise Pascal, that towering seventeenth-century mathematician, about his affirmation of "the God of Abraham, the God of Isaac, the God of Jacob, not of philosophers and scholars" (*Dieu d'Abraham, Dieu d'Isaac, Dieu de Jacob, non des philosophes et des savants*). Modern atheism is in many instances the product not so much of antireligion as of religion's replacement of the God of Abraham with the god of the philosophers, and the subsequent rejection of that *ersatz* god by other philosophers. René Descartes determined that he would not accept as true anything that could be reasonably doubted, and Christians set about to prove that the existence of God could not be reasonably doubted. Thus did the defenders of religion set faith against the doubt (understood as rational inquiry) that is, for most thoughtful people, a necessary part of faith.

Talk about affirming or denying the *existence* of God is itself problematic. That way of talking can suggest to the unwary that God is one existent among other existents, one entity among other entities, one actor among other actors, whose actions must conform to standards that we have determined in advance are appropriate to being God. The transcendent, the ineffable, that which surpasses our ability to conceive or speak, the biblical God who acts in history, was too often tamed and domesticated in order to meet the philosophers' job description for the post of God. Not surprisingly, the philosophers determined that the candidates recommended by the friends of religion did not qualify for the post.

The American part of this story is well told by James Turner of the University of Michigan. "The natural parents of modern unbelief," Turner writes, "turn out to have been the guardians of belief." Many thinking people came at last "to realize that it was religion, not science or social change, that gave birth to unbelief. Having made God more and more like man—intellectually, morally, emotionally—the shapers of religion made it feasible to abandon God, to believe simply in man." Turner's judgment of liberal religion is relentless: "In trying to adapt their religious beliefs to socioeconomic change, to new moral challenges, to novel problems of knowledge, to the tightening standards of science, the defenders of God slowly strangled Him. If anyone is to be arraigned for deicide, it is not Charles Darwin but his adversary Bishop Samuel Wilberforce, not the godless Robert Ingersoll but the godly Beecher family." The Beecher family refers, of course, to Lyman Beecher and his formidable children, Henry Ward Beecher and Harriet Beecher Stowe, author of *Uncle Tom's Cabin.*

In response to that variety of liberal Protestantism, H. L. Mencken observed that "the chief contribution of Protestantism to human thought is its massive proof that God is a bore." That is unfair, of course—and Mencken was usually unfair—but it is not untouched by truth. The god that was trimmed, accommodated, and retooled in order to be deemed respectable by the "modern mind" was increasingly uninteresting, because unnecessary. Dietrich Bonhoeffer, the Lutheran theologian who was executed on the direct order of Hitler weeks before the end of the war, described that god as a "god of the gaps" who was invoked to fill in those pieces of reality that human knowledge and control had not yet mastered. H. Richard Niebuhr's well-known and withering depiction of the gospel of liberal Christianity is to the point: "A God without wrath brought men without sin into a kingdom without judgment through the ministrations of a Christ without a Cross." Absent our sin and God's judgment and redemption, it is not surprising that people came to dismiss the idea of God, not because it is implausible but because it is superfluous, and, yes, boring.

There is also the more determined materialist who asserts that there simply is nothing and can be nothing outside a closed and all-encompassing reality of matter in motion. This was the position of the late and unlamented "dialectical materialism" of communism. It is the position of some scientists today, especially those in the biological sciences who are wedded to Darwinism not just as a scientific theory but as a comprehensive belief system. In Chapter 3 we discussed the incoherence, the internal contradiction, in believing that all reality, including human consciousness, is utterly determined by natural forces over which we have no control and, at the same time, claiming that we are free to make decisions—including the decision to believe that all reality is determined by natural forces over which we have no control. People are, of course, free to be determinists, even if they are determined to deny their freedom in embracing that unfortunate philosophy.

Perhaps more commonly, one encounters varieties of logical positivism that hold that since assertions about

God are not empirically verifiable—or, for that matter, falsifiable—they are simply meaningless. In a similar vein, analytical philosophers would instruct us that "God talk" is, quite precisely, non-sense. This is not atheism in the usual sense, since it claims that denying God is as much nonsense as affirming God. It is atheism, however, in the original sense of *a-theos,* of being without God. Then there is the much more radical position that denies not only the possibility of truth claims about God but the possibility of claims about truth at all—at least as "truth" has usually been understood in our history. A prominent proponent of this argument in America is the late Richard Rorty, whom we met earlier in connection with his belief in the truth that America is the object of our deepest devotion.

Rorty is sometimes portrayed, and in fact he portrayed himself, as something of an eccentric gadfly. But along with Jacques Derrida, Michel Foucault, and other Heideggerian epigones of Nietzsche, Rorty was the guru of an academic establishment of great influence in our intellectual culture. Here we encounter the apostles of a relativism that denies it is relativism because it denies that there is any alternative to relativism, and therefore the term "relativism" is meaningless. They are radically antifoundationalist. That is to say, they contend that there are no conclusive arguments underlying our assertions, except the conclusive argument that there are no conclusive arguments. To put it much too briefly, but not, I think, inaccurately, "truth" (in quotes) is what the relevant community of discourse agrees to say is true.

The goal, in this way of thinking, is self-actualization, indeed self-creation. The successful life is the life lived as a *novum,* an autobiography that has escaped the "used vocabularies" of the past. This disposition has its academic strongholds in literary criticism and sectors of philosophy, but it underlies assumptions that are very widespread in our intellectual culture. In some variations it is frankly asserted that arguments claiming to deal with truth are but disguised stratagems for the exercise of the will to power. Whether the issue is gender, sexual orientation, class struggle, or race, we are told that the challenge is to change the ideational "power structure" presently controlled by oppressors who disingenuously try to protect the status quo by making appeals to objective truth and inter-subjective reason.

But are people who embrace such views atheists? Many of them brush aside the question as "not serious," for the theism upon which atheism depends is, in their view, not serious. As with relativism and irrationality, so also with atheism—the words only make sense in relation to the opposites against which they are posed. Of course, privately, or for purposes of a particular community, any words might be deemed useful. One might even find it meaningful to speak about "nature and nature's God," as does the Declaration of Independence. People can be permitted to talk that way, so long as they understand that such talk has no public purchase. Rorty's "liberal ironist" can employ any vocabulary, no matter how fantastical, so long as he does not insist that it is true in a way that makes a claim upon others or limits their novel vocabularies. I will return to Rorty later, for his thought is, I believe, very important in understanding our public confusions.

Over the past several decades we have witnessed many variations on what is called "deconstructionism."

The premise—one must never say *foundation*!—of this way of thinking is that what we call reality is socially constructed, and is typically constructed in ways that disguise or try to justify the unjust exercise of power by the unjustly advantaged. The great intellectual task, therefore, is to deconstruct these oppressive structures of deceit. There is indeed irony in the fact that some who think of themselves as theists eagerly embrace deconstructionism's operative atheism. The reason for this is that among the things that deconstructionism deconstructs is an older form of Enlightenment rationalism that excluded religion from the company of rational discourse. By deconstructing that narrow and exclusive type of rationalism, it is said, deconstructionism gives religion "a place at the table," along with myriad other "alternative" constructions of reality.

Christians and Jews who are touchingly pleased to have a place at the table might well ask themselves whether the price of admission is not too high. A place at the table is secured by agreeing not to make any inconvenient claims about what is true or false. The old Enlightenment rationalism, while cripplingly constricted in its idea of reason, at least insisted that what is at stake is the *truth* about things. On that we alien citizens insistently agree. We think we have a much more comprehensive understanding of the truth about things than do such rationalists, but, to the extent that they and we agree in refusing to put sneer quotes around the word *truth,* we are allies.

Our question of whether atheists can be good citizens is complicated by a circumstance in which it is not always clear who is and who is not an atheist. Today's cultural scene is awash in what are described as "new spiritualities." A recent anthology featuring "America's new spiritual voices" includes contributions promoting witchcraft, ecological mysticism, devotion to sundry gods and goddesses, and something advertising itself as "Zen physio-psychoanalysis." All are deemed to be usable vocabularies for the creation of the self. Is a Zen physio-psychoanalyst an atheist? If the Christian understanding of faith in God is the measure, I expect so. To be sure, there are many people who refuse to answer the "God question" one way or another. They frequently describe themselves as "agnostics." "Agnosticism" can refer to a provisional point of uncertainty in wrestling with a question of ultimate importance. Very commonly, however, when people identify themselves as agnostics, it is a reflection of intellectual laziness. They not only have no need of Laplace's "hypothesis"; they have decided not to think about it, or at least not think about it very hard.

There are also curious twists and turns under ostensibly orthodox Christian auspices. References to transcendent realities are sometimes conflated with, and sometimes subordinated to, social agendas of great variety. In this instance, belief in God is *useful* for achieving other purposes. Underlying such distortions is the greatest of all category mistakes—mistaking the creature for the Creator. Cardinal Avery Dulles tells of speaking in a Catholic parish where a large banner at the front of the church declared, "God is Other People." He wished that he had with him a magic marker so that he could put an emphatic comma after the word "Other." That comma makes all the difference: "God is Other, People." Whether under Christian or non-Christian auspices, many of the "spiritualities" in contemporary culture would seem to be elaborately religionized forms of atheism.

There are very impressive arguments made today against the idea of rationality upon which most Enlightenment atheism was based. One thinks, for instance, of Alasdair MacIntyre, and especially of his *Three Rival Versions of Moral Inquiry.* MacIntyre's criticism is directed at a view of rationality that claims to be universal, disinterested, autonomous, and free from the authority of tradition. MacIntyre contends that there are *traditions of rationality* in conflict. He makes a strong case for the tradition associated with Thomas Aquinas with its synthesis of Aristotle and Augustine. He then joins forces with some "postmodernists" in debunking the hegemonic pretensions of the autonomous and foundational rationality that has for so long dominated our intellectual culture. After the great debunking, the cards of rival traditions will be put on the table and we can then have at it. Presumably, the tradition that can provide the best account of reality—or persuade the players with greatest influence—will win out. More likely, the rivalry will continue indefinitely, but with a more candid acknowledgment that no one philosophical player has an exclusive claim on being rational.

In referring to this as a game, I do not suggest that it is a frivolous undertaking. But it does have a game-like quality, with moves and countermoves in the service of intellectual strategies. And, like all serious games, it entails risks. It is important to expose the fallacious value-neutrality of those who claim to argue from a tradition-free and autonomous rationality. That exposure can level the field for the arguments of eminently reasonable theism. It can also invite into the discussion a Nietzschian "will to power" that is determined to set the rules, including rules designed to preclude the return of the gods or God in a manner that claims public acknowledgment. For one tradition of reason (for example, Thomism) to form an alliance, or even a temporary coalition, with unreason in order to undo another tradition of reason (for example, value-neutral Enlightenment rationality) is a perilous tactic.

Yet something like that may be the future of our intellectual culture. In our universities, Christians, Jews, and, increasingly, Muslims will be free to contend for their truths, just as Marxists, Nietzschians, utilitarians of all varieties, and devotees of the Great Earth Goddess are free to contend for theirs. It is a matter of equal-opportunity propaganda. Every party will be permitted to contend for their truths so long as they acknowledge that they are *their* truths, and not *the* truth. Each will be permitted to propagandize, each will *have* to propagandize, if it is to hold its own, because it is acknowledged that there is no common ground for the alternative to propaganda, which is reasonable persuasion. As is the way with games, we do not know how this one will turn out. There is reason to fear, however, that theism, when it plays by the rules of the atheism of unreason, will be gravely compromised. The method becomes the message. Contemporary Christian theology already provides too many instances of the peddling of truths that are not in service to the truth of the God of Israel manifest in the eternal *logos*.

We have touched briefly, then, on some of the many faces of atheism—of living and thinking *a-theos*, without God or the gods. There is the atheism of the early Christians, who posited God against the gods. There is the atheism of Enlightenment rationalists, who, committed to presumably undoubtable certainty, rejected the god whom religionists designed to fit that criterion. There is the practical atheism of Laplace, who had no need of "that hypothesis" in order to get on with what he had to do. There is the weary atheism of those who grew bored with liberalism's god created in the image and likeness of good liberals. There is the more thorough atheism of Nietzschian will to power. And, finally, there is the atheism of putative theists who peddle religious truths that are true for you, if you find it useful to believe them true.

Can these atheists be good citizens? It depends, I suppose, on what is meant by good citizenship. We may safely assume that the great majority of those who say they are atheists abide by the laws and pay their taxes, and they may even be congenial and helpful neighbors. When some years ago I publicly raised the question of whether atheists could be good citizens, the gifted cartoonist and author Jules Feiffer responded with a full-page cartoon in *The Nation*. He cleverly depicted a series of scandals in which clergy, both Protestant and Catholic, were caught doing very bad things. His implicit counter-question was whether Christians could be good citizens. Fair enough. In its purely human dimensions, religion is decidedly impure. It is as riddled through with rascality as any other human enterprise. That, as the lawyers say, can be stipulated.

We can go further, however, and acknowledge that an atheist can be an exceedingly moral person, a person more morally serious than many Christians are. He can be moral also with respect to the virtue of intellectual honesty. One cannot *prove* definitively and beyond possible doubt that God is. At the same time, one cannot *prove* that he is not. This leads many to a position of agnosticism rather than atheism. Agnosticism, as I said, is often the stance of the intellectually lazy, of those who are not prepared to think the matter through to a conclusion. However wrongheaded his conclusion, there can be an element of intellectual and moral seriousness in the atheist's readiness to take a stand on this greatest of all matters.

Some might be surprised that Pope Benedict XVI agrees. In his 2007 encyclical *Spe Salvi* (Saved in Hope), he writes:

> The atheism of the nineteenth and twentieth centuries is—in its origins and aims—a type of moralism. It is a protest against the injustices of the world and of world history. A world marked by so much injustice, innocent suffering, and cynicism of power cannot be the work of a good God. A God with responsibility for such a world would not be a just God, much less a good God. It is for the sake of morality that this God has to be contested.

We will later return to this argument advanced by Benedict.

Father Raniero Cantalamessa, preacher to the papal household, takes our question from a different angle:

> The world of today knows a new category of people: the atheists in good faith, those who live painfully the situation of the silence of God, who do not believe in God but do not boast about it; rather they experience the ex-

> istential anguish and the lack of meaning of everything: They too, in their own way, live in the dark night of the spirit. Albert Camus called them "the saints without God." The mystics exist above all for them; they are their travel and table companions. Like Jesus, they "sat down at the table of sinners and ate with them" (see Luke 15:2). This explains the passion with which certain atheists, once converted, pore over the writings of the mystics: Claudel, Bernanos, the two Maritains, L. Bloy, the writer J. K. Huysmans and so many others over the writings of Angela of Foligno; T. S. Eliot over those of Julian of Norwich. There they find again the same scenery that they had left, but this time illuminated by the sun. . . . The word "atheist" can have an active and a passive meaning. It can indicate someone who rejects God, but also one who—at least so it seems to him—is rejected by God. In the first case, it is a blameworthy atheism (when it is not in good faith), in the second an atheism of sorrow or of expiation.

There are atheists and then there are atheists.

The question of whether atheists can be good citizens is hardly original with me, and it engages concerns that go beyond individual rectitude or moral and intellectual seriousness. As a generality, can people who do not acknowledge that they are accountable to a truth higher than the self, a truth that is not dependent upon the self, really be trusted? John Locke, among many other worthies, thought not. However confused these thinkers may have been in their theology, they were sure that the social contract was based upon nature, upon the way the world *really is*. They were convinced that respect for a higher judgment, even an eternal judgment, was essential to citizenship.

It followed, in their view, that an atheist could not be trusted to be a good citizen, and therefore could not be a citizen at all. Locke is rightly celebrated as a champion of religious toleration, but not of irreligion. "Those are not at all to be tolerated who deny the being of a God," he writes. "Promises, covenants, and oaths, which are the bonds of human society, can have no hold upon an atheist. The taking away of God, though but even in thought, dissolves all." *The taking away of God dissolves all.* Every text becomes pretext, every interpretation a strategy, and every oath a deceit. So said John Locke, whom some view as the premier intellectual guide of the American founding. Admittedly, Locke also thought that Catholics could not be good citizens. But that, he said, was for the very different reason that they owed a higher allegiance to a foreign potentate, the pope in Rome.

James Madison, in his famed *Memorial and Remonstrance* of 1785, also addressed the question of atheists as citizens. It is frequently forgotten that, for Madison and the other founders, religious freedom was an inalienable right that presupposed an inalienable duty. Madison wrote, for instance: "It is the duty of every man to render to the Creator such homage and such only as he believes to be acceptable to him. This duty is precedent, both in order of time and in degree of obligation, to the claims of Civil Society."

Then follows this passage that could hardly be more pertinent to the question that prompts our present reflection:

> Before any man can be considered as a member of Civil Society, he must be considered as a subject of the Governour of the Universe: And if a member of Civil Society, who enters into any subordinate Association, must always do it with a reservation of his duty to the General Authority; much more must every man who becomes a member of any particular Civil Society, do it with a saving of his allegiance to the Universal Sovereign.

That captures an important part of what it means to be an alien citizen in the city of man.

Moreover, in the period of the American founding, state constitutions could and did exclude atheists from public office. It is well worth recalling, however, how much the founders had in common with respect to religious and philosophical beliefs. While a few were sympathetic to milder or stronger versions of Deism, and some were rigorous Calvinists in the Puritan tradition, almost all assumed a clearly Christian, and clearly Protestant, construal of reality. In the language of philosophical discourse, the founders were "moral realists," which is to say they assumed the reality of a good not of their own construction. This is amply demonstrated from many sources, not least the Declaration and the Constitution, and especially the Preamble of the latter.

The Constitution of the United States is sometimes described as "godless," and it is true that God is not mentioned; religion is mentioned only with respect to "free exercise" (the First Amendment) and the rule against a "religious test" as a requirement for holding public office (Article VI). While the Declaration is more religiously specific, the Preamble to the Constitution resonates with value-laden assumptions about the right ordering of this *novus ordo seclorum:*

> We the people of the United States, in order to form a more perfect union, establish justice, insure domestic tranquility, provide for the common defense, promote the general welfare, and secure the blessings of liberty to ourselves and our posterity, do ordain and establish this Constitution for the United States of America.

One frequently hears it said that this constitutional order is entirely "procedural." It steers clear of any reference to "substantive goods," contenting itself with addressing "means" rather than "ends." But that reading of the Constitution cannot survive an honest examination of the Preamble, which explicitly sets forth the purpose, as in *ends,* of the entire exercise. This is simply to acknowledge the obvious, namely, that the Constitution is a political document. And again, the classical understanding of politics is that of free persons deliberating the question, *How ought we to order our life together*? The *ought* in that definition clearly signals that politics is in its nature, if not always in its practice, a moral enterprise. Having set forth the goods and blessings they desire to secure for themselves and their posterity, the founders, acting in the name of "We the people of the United States," then go on to specify the means by which they will deliberate and decide how this people ought to order their life together.

In 1787 and also today, the questions of "oughtness" are moral questions. The very vocabulary of politics is inescapably moral. With respect to innumerable issues, we debate what is right and what is wrong, what is fair and what is unfair, what serves and what disserves the common good. In any society, moral judgments draw upon the deepest beliefs and convictions held by the people of that society. In America and most of the world, those beliefs and convictions are inseparable from religious traditions. This may seem self-evident to most readers, but in fact it touches on questions that continue to be hotly contested.

It is true that the Constitution establishes a secular order of government. The word "secular" is from the Latin *saeculum,* which means the present time. To say that this government is secular is to say that it is for the present time; it is a temporal order. It is for the city of man, not the City of God. The American founders did not establish this constitutional order to be a church, although for some secularists it may be the closest thing they have to a church. This constitutional order is temporal, provisional, for the time being. It is not the New Jerusalem. Nor is it, as the Church of Jesus Christ claims to be, the sacramental prolepsis of the New Jerusalem. Within the cosmic scheme of things, it is a modest enterprise. Yes, the founders hoped it would be, as the Great Seal of the United States declares, a *novus ordo seclorum*—a new order for the ages. But they also regularly spoke of this political order as an "experiment," and experiments can succeed or fail. In terms of longevity and adaptability, America is the most successful political experiment in human history. But it is still for the time being.

It is a secular order, but it is not, as the proponents of *secularism* would have it, an order designed to exclude religion and religiously grounded moral discernment from our common life. Such an exclusion is impossible if we understand politics as the task of democratically deliberating and deciding how we ought to order our life together. And such an exclusion is manifestly not what the founders intended. There continues to be much, and sometimes rancorous, disagreement about religion and the founding. There is no shortage of writers who, allowing that the founders typically employed religious language to describe their undertaking, claim that they did so only or mainly for political reasons. As in Edward Gibbon's description of imperial Rome, the people thought religion true, the philosophers thought it false, and the rulers thought it useful. This is, to put it delicately, a very cynical view of the American founding, and it simply does not comport with the facts.

Historians have shown that the experience of the seventeenth-century Puritan settlement with religious persecution in the Old World was vibrantly alive in the minds of the eighteenth-century founders. What came to be called the "separation of church and state"—Jefferson's phrase, which, of course, is not in the Constitution—was designed to protect religion, both private and public, from control by the state. The first liberty of the First Amendment—the free exercise of religion—marked the first time in the annals of history that a government surrendered its right to control what its people believed, in the full awareness that the government depended on the consent of the governed. It was, and it is, an audacious experiment. Likewise, other scholars have spelled out in illuminating detail the ways in which the formative ideas of the founders were explicitly drawn from Jewish and Christian ideas of human nature, historical purpose, and moral judgment. There is today a growing literature, both scholarly and popular, that counters the secularist distortion of the founding that long held sway in textbooks from grade school through graduate school.

Countering a distortion runs the risk of producing a counter-distortion. It is not true that all the founders, or even almost all, were devout, Bible-believing Christians along the lines we associate with twenty-first-century evangelical Christians. Evangelical Christians who lack a vibrant ecclesiology and are therefore inclined to turn the nation into their church are sometimes tempted to embrace this counter-distortion. The result is a hyper-patriotism in which people are able to bow the knee to the nation while telling themselves that this is not idolatry, which it is. The caricature of the founders promoted by radical secularists is to be rejected, but it should not be replaced by another caricature. The founders did live, after all, in the eighteenth century, which is not for nothing called the Age of Enlightenment.

This does not mean that the founders were Deists, if by Deism one means the idea of God as a celestial watchmaker who wound up the universe and then withdrew to let it run on its own. It is true that many European intellectuals of the time could be accurately described as Deists, and, when addressing European audiences, American leaders sometimes adopted elements of the Deist vocabulary. When speaking to Americans, however, they spoke the language of the Bible, and from their own words, both public and private, it is evident that they lived in an intellectual universe shaped by the Protestant tradition in its several Calvinist and revivalist varieties.

Even Thomas Jefferson, so frequently cited as *the* authority on religion and the founding, was not much of a Deist. And, of course, he was off in France and did not participate in the debates that produced the Constitution. This puts a severe crimp in the argument that he is the authority on the "original meaning" of that document and its amendments. As eccentric, and eccentrically brilliant, as Jefferson frequently was, he seemed to share the Jewish-Christian worldview common to the founders. Far from believing that God was a watchmaker who wound up the world and then let it run by itself, Jefferson in his Second Inaugural Address professed the need for "the favor of that Being in whose hands we are, who led our fathers, as Israel of old, from their native land and planted them in a country flowing with all the necessaries and comforts of life, who has covered our infancy with his providence and our riper years with his wisdom and power." This is a God very engaged in the space and time of his creation.

To be sure, this is the same Jefferson who took scissors and paste to the four gospels, which resulted in *The Life and Morals of Jesus of Nazareth,* usually called "The Jefferson Bible." Although he excised from the gospels crucial elements of Christian orthodoxy that were not to his liking, his bowdlerized text is compatible with the distinctly non-Deistic beliefs expressed in his Second Inaugural Address and elsewhere in his writings. It is also worth noting that he never published *Life and Morals,* knowing full well that it would scandalize his more orthodox colleagues and countrymen. Also, perhaps, because he was not sure of its adequacy as an account of his own beliefs. As president, the same Jefferson who coined the phrase "wall of separation between church and state" thought it only fitting that he should attend Sunday services that were then held, interestingly enough, in the chamber of the House of Representatives.

Benjamin Franklin is another who is frequently described as a Deist. He was lionized in France and got along swimmingly with the intelligentsia there, but the fact that he was celebrated by Deists and atheists does not mean he was one of them. At the Constitutional Convention of 1787, the elderly Franklin said, "The longer I live, the more convincing proofs I see of this truth—that God governs in the affairs of men. And if a sparrow cannot fall to the ground without his notice, is it probable that an empire cannot rise without his aid?" This understanding fits very nicely the words *Annuit Coeptis*—"He has favored our undertaking"—inscribed on the Great Seal of the United States in 1782.

Jefferson and Franklin are the authorities routinely invoked by revisionists who would minimize or erase the religion factor in the American founding. Theirs is not an easy task. We have already heard from James Madison on the "precedent" duty the citizen owes to God, and it would be tedious to cite similar statements by Robert Morris, Alexander Hamilton, Patrick Henry, John Dickenson, Daniel Carroll, and others who were, so to speak, present at the creation. Abundant documentation is to be found in the books mentioned earlier.

Even in such a brief discussion of religion and the founding, we cannot overlook the familiar words of George Washington's Farewell Address upon completing his second term as the first president. The address, composed with the help of Hamilton and others, is a brilliant *tour d'horizon* of the history, convictions, and institutions that were part of the American experiment.

Toward the end of the address, Washington speaks of that which is essential to the entire enterprise:

> Of all the dispositions and habits which lead to political prosperity, religion and morality are indispensable supports. In vain would that man claim the tribute of patriotism, who should labor to subvert these great pillars of human happiness, these firmest props of the duties of men and citizens. The mere politician, equally with the pious man, ought to respect and to cherish them. A volume could not trace all their connections with private and public felicity. Let it simply be asked: Where is the security for property, for reputation, for life, if the sense of religious obligation desert the oaths which are the instruments of investigation in courts of justice? And let us with caution indulge the supposition that morality can be maintained without religion. Whatever may be conceded to the influence of refined education on minds of peculiar structure, reason and experience both forbid us to expect that national morality can prevail in exclusion of religious principle.

The supposition that Washington said should be indulged with caution—that morality can be maintained without religion—has today become secularist orthodoxy. And, of course, Washington quickly added that reason and experience forbid us to think the supposition is true, at least with respect to public morality. In any event, the supposition has never been put to the test in America, which almost all agree is an incorrigibly and pervasively religious society. That does not prevent those who are the product of "refined education on minds of peculiar structure" from trying to expunge religion from the defining story of the American experiment.

It is perfectly understandable that people who want to shape the future of that story are eager to lay claim to the constituting moment by which it is defined. That such claims and counterclaims will continue with no end in sight is evidence of the vitality of the experiment. Even those who are no friends of the jurisprudence based on "original meaning" have no choice but to present themselves as advocates of the original meaning of the constituting moment, no matter how much their proposals may deviate from the intentions of the founders. In the absence of a claimed continuity with the constituting moment, such proposed futures cannot believably present themselves as the future of the *American* story and thus have slight chance of gaining a hearing from a people who are stubbornly determined to be Americans.

We have touched on the influence of John Locke and his understanding of the "social contract." The founders' notion of the social contract was not a truncated and mechanistic contrivance of calculated self-interest. This is not to say that self-interest was ignored. James Madison's contribution to *The Federalist* was a masterful treatment of the ways in which self-interest and conflicting self-interests—which are, given human nature, inevitable—can, in a republican order, serve the interests of all. Or, to put it more modestly, conflicting self-interests need not be what today is called a zero-sum game, and need not destroy the constitutional order that all have an interest in maintaining.

In the larger vision of the founders, the social contract is as importantly a *compact,* and that compact is premised upon a sense of covenantal purpose guiding this *novus ordo seclorum,* just as Washington, Jefferson, Franklin, Adams, and the others said. The understanding of a covenant encompassing the contract was, in a time of supreme testing, brought to full and magisterial articulation by Abraham Lincoln. Through the fratricidal bloodletting of a civil war that took more than 600,000 lives, there was born a yet deeper understanding of a constitution that represented not a deal struck but, as Lincoln said at Gettysburg, "a nation so conceived and so dedicated."

In such a nation, an atheist can be a citizen, but he cannot be a good citizen. A good citizen does more than abide by the laws. A good citizen is able to give an account, a morally compelling account, of the regime of which he is part—and to do so in continuity with the constituting moment and subsequent history of that regime. He is able to justify its defense against its enemies, and to convincingly recommend its virtues to citizens of the next generation so that they, in turn, can transmit the order of government to citizens yet unborn. This regime of liberal democracy, of republican self-governance, is not self-evidently good and just. An account must be given. Reasons must be given. They must be reasons that draw authority from that which is higher than ourselves, from that which transcends us, from that to which we are precedently, ultimately, obliged.

Again, there are atheists and then there are atheists. There are the morally earnest who feel driven to their grim conclusion, including those whom Albert Camus calls "saints without God." They are reluctant atheists who may respect, even if they cannot in conscience affirm, the truths by which this political order is constructed. Then there are the "new atheists," who exult in publicly assaulting the religiously grounded foundations and aspirations of this order. The product of what Washington called "refined education on minds of peculiar structure," they glory in the indulgence of the transgressive and measure their presumed superiority by their success in scandalizing the devout. It is a poignant spectacle, and apparently a lucrative enterprise, although it appears they are not in it for anything so innocent as the money. The anger and palpable malevolence, sometimes laced with acidic wit, calls for a deeper psychological analysis than can be ventured here.

Those who adhere to the God of Abraham, Isaac, Jacob, and Jesus turn out to be the best citizens. Those who were once called "atheists" are now the most persuasive defenders not of the gods but of the good reasons for this regime of ordered liberty. They are that not *despite* the fact that their loyalty to this *polis* is qualified by a higher loyalty, but *because* of it. Among the best of the good reasons they give in defending this regime is that it makes a sharply limited claim upon the loyalty of its citizens. The ultimate allegiance of the faithful is not to the regime or to its constituting texts, but to the City of God and the sacred texts that guide our path toward that destination. We are dual citizens in a regime that, as Madison and others underscored, was designed for such duality. When the political order forgets itself and reestablishes the gods of the *polis,* even if it does so in the name of liberal democracy, these citizens have no choice but to run the risk of once again being called "atheists."

The American experiment in constitutional democracy was not conceived and dedicated by those who today call themselves "atheists," and it cannot be conceived and dedicated anew by such citizens. In times of testing—and every time is a time of testing for this experiment in ordered liberty—a morally convincing account must be given. One may ask, Convincing to whom? One obvious answer in a democracy, although not the only answer, is that it must be convincing to a majority of citizens. Minorities, including the minority of atheists, are assiduously to be protected in their legal right to dissent. It is the responsibility of their fellow citizens to give a moral account—an account that atheists cannot give—of why that is the case. Giving such an account in continuity with the truths by which this political order was constituted is required of good citizens, not least because those who cannot give such an account depend on others who can.

V

An Age of Irony

WE HAVE NO alternative to this moment of time that is Babylon. More accurately, we have no *presently available* alternative. Babylon is for all time short of *the* alternative which is the promised New Jerusalem. Babylon is life in the realm of what Saint Augustine calls *libido dominandi*—the realm of the earthly city ruled by the lust for power and glory. For centuries Christians have prayed, "Thy kingdom come, thy will be done." And it is possible Christians will be praying that prayer for centuries more.

We live "between the times"—between the time of the new world inaugurated in the death and resurrection of Jesus and that new world consummated in his return to establish the Kingdom of God. Such are the images and such is the language by which Christians situate themselves in a world between the times, a *world of the meanwhile,* as they await the vindication of their hope. In his 2007 encyclical on hope, *Spe Salvi,* Pope Benedict notes an inscription found in the ancient ruins of Rome:

In nihil ab nihilo quam cito recidimus—"How quickly we fall back from nothing to nothing."

Not so with Christians, writes Benedict: "When the *Letter to the Hebrews* says that Christians here on earth do not have a permanent homeland but seek one which lies in the future, this does not mean that they live only for the future: present society is recognized by Christians as an exile; they belong to a new society that is the goal of their common pilgrimage and is anticipated in the course of that pilgrimage."

Although all Christians are in exile, some are more at home in their exile than others. And some times and places are more home-like than others. This can be a great comfort, and a great temptation. The temptation is to unpack, settle down in the present, and forget about the pilgrimage. Therein lies the ambiguity of the period we call *Christendom,* which runs roughly from the fourth century to the sixteenth. A contemporary scholar, Augustine Thompson, catches this very nicely in his luminous book *Cities of God,* a study of Italian communes from 1125 to 1325: "By the thirteenth century, immersion in the font of the city baptistery made the baptized a citizen of the commune. It created a bond like siblinghood among all those baptized there. Dante, meeting Cacciaguida in heaven, heard his ancestor recall his rebirth at Florence's beloved San Giovanni; the baptismal bond had made them fellow citizens." Thompson quotes Dante:

To so restful and so true
A life as citizens, to such beautiful
citizenship, to such a faithful household,

Mary, invoked with loud cries, gave me;
and in your ancient baptistery,
at once I became both Christian and Cacciaguida.

Christendom sometimes provided an almost seamless fusion of the city of man with the City of God. It was exile without alienation, as though nature and grace converged in providing a fitting home here and an assured graduation, in due course, from the earthly city to the New Jerusalem. To be sure, that is an ideal depiction of Christendom, which we know was accompanied also by the yearnings and terrors common to the human condition. In any event, that Christendom is no longer available to Christians today, and it is hardly possible to imagine how it could ever be again.

For most of the faithful through most of history, exile has a harder edge. The pain of dislocation is more deeply felt. For the psalmist it was the sorrow of singing the songs of Zion in a foreign land. For the Old Testament Daniel and his companions Shadrach, Meshach, and Abednego, it was making themselves useful to foreign authorities, but only up to the point of not surrendering their souls. They chose death over idolatry. Also today, those who know they live far from Zion experience a world made strange.

Some choose accommodation—up to a point, praying that they will recognize that point when it comes. Some strive to engage and transform the world where they are, hoping to make it less strange, knowing it will always fall pitifully short of the city to which they are called. For yet others, fidelity in exile is the course of subversion and even insurrection. Witness the liberation theologies of our time and all times. Then there are those who deliberately, and often at great sacrifice, choose to create enclaves of fidelity, outposts of the promised Kingdom, islands of Christendom in the absence of Christendom. Thus a dynamic that is at the core of the monastic tradition. Thus a growing number of Christian parents today who, through home schooling and other exertions, strive to make the family a haven from a heartless world. Faithfulness in exile takes many forms.

It is not only Christians who devise strategies to cope with homelessness. Also those who do not credit the rumor of a home elsewhere try to secure tolerable accommodations in a less-than-hospitable world. For many of these, irony comes to the rescue, sort of. Irony is a form of distancing; of protecting oneself from disappointment by not hoping for too much; of worldly-wise defense against being taken in; of skepticism as an armor against naïveté; of debunking truths that threaten to inconveniently oblige; of an amused posture of superiority to a world unworthy of one's most singular self. We speak of "the age of this" and "the age of that," and our cultural moment has been called, not without reason, an age of irony. Our humor is ironic; our histories are ironic. It is considered a compliment to say a writer has a fine sense of irony.

Irony takes several forms. There is Socratic irony, in which one pretends ignorance and an eagerness to learn from others with the purpose of exposing, through apparently naïve questioning, the falsity of their ideas. There is also dramatic irony, in which the playwright lets the audience in on the incongruities not understood by the players. Irony is frequently in the mode of playfulness, even a bitter playfulness, aimed at displaying what is ludicrous, incongruous, and pretentious in a world of which one cannot help being part but to which one is determined not to be captive. Yes, says the ironist, see how fatuous and false is the world of which I am part, but see also the panache with which I rise above it, my amused toleration of those who take it all so very seriously.

Modernity—including the heightened modernism originating in the arts and now called postmodernity—is not hospitable to a Christian way of being in the world. Some Christians try to sympathetically engage our culture in the hope of transforming it; others hunker down with their own kind to wait out the time of exile; yet others choose the liberationist path of insurrection, whether by frontal assault or guerrilla warfare. And some elect the course of demonstrating their ironic superiority to a world that does not tire of reminding them that they are aliens.

It is an understatement to say that much of what we call modernity has not been Christian-friendly. Voltaire took pleasure in publishing the last will and testament of his friend Jean Messelier, who declared, "I should like to see, and this will be the last and the most ardent of my desires, I should like to see the last king strangled with the guts of the last priest." The antireligious passion of certain streams of the Enlightenment is well known. Indeed, it is so well known that, in many circles, the Enlightenment is equated with militant secularism. The legacy of that Enlightenment is still encountered in mental habits that, in a taken-for-granted manner, pit reason against faith, evidence against revelation, and enlightenment against superstition—and most mightily against religious superstition.

When Enlightenment figures were not overtly hostile to religion, their arguments frequently resulted in consigning religion to a ghetto of privatized subjectivity. In "What Is Enlightenment?" Immanuel Kant made a sharp distinction between public and private reason. Public reason is the critical and analytical thing that scholars do for an enlightened public, while private reason reinforces what is necessary to sustain the religious and civil order. Only public reason qualifies as enlightenment, meaning the pursuit of free inquiry independent from the institutions and traditions of authority. "Our age," Kant declared, "is, in especial degree, the age of criticism, and to criticism everything must submit."

Our civilization's story as told in this Enlightenment vein is still today offered in the casual manner of relating the self-evident. To cite but one of innumerable instances, there is Peter Gay's *The Enlightenment: An Interpretation.* The great thing about the Enlightenment, Gay says, was the dawning of the way of reason that displaced the beliefs of "traditional religion," which had been dependent solely upon faith. "The great religions of antiquity," Gay writes, "all bear this character: they were not reasoned about; they did not require proof and hence could not be disproved."

The distinguished historian of Christianity Robert Louis Wilken points out that such cavalier claims are disproved by even a cursory acquaintance with the religious traditions. He notes that Judah ha-Nasi codified the Jewish laws in the Mishnah, the Amoraiim added their critical debates and recorded them in the Talmud, and Rashi and Tosaphists joined the discussion, all of which was put in the margins of the text, which enables the contemporary student to take part in debates that have been going on for centuries. "Similarly," Wilken says, "Augustine read Paul and Plotinus (who had read Plato), Peter Lombard organized and codified the views of Augustine and other early Christian thinkers, Thomas Aquinas read Lombard, Francisco de Suarez read Thomas, and in our day Etienne Gilson read Augustine, Lombard, Thomas, and Suarez."

"Religious scholarship," Wilken writes, "has never been simply a matter of copying texts, of parsing sentences, of analyzing and explaining words and phrases." He cites Peter Abelard, who wrote, "For the first key to wisdom is called *interrogatio,* diligent and unceasing questioning. . . . By doubting we are led to inquiry; and from inquiry we perceive the truth." In the Middle Ages, Jews, Christians, and Muslims were engaged in a three-cornered discussion, or, better, a four-cornered discussion, since all were in conversation with Aristotle. It was a rigorously critical discussion, thoroughly rational, although not what we would today call rationalistic. The imperative of reason was well stated by Augustine: "No one believes anything unless one first thought it to be believable. . . . Everything which is believed should be believed after thought has preceded. . . . Not everyone who thinks believes, since many think in order not to believe; but everyone who believes thinks." In this chapter, we look at the way Richard Rorty thought in order not to believe. His way of "liberal ironism" has been, willy nilly, adopted by innumerable contemporaries who have never heard of Richard Rorty. But in order to understand that way it is first necessary, as he insists, to situate it within a brief consideration of intellectual history.

In the Enlightenment tradition, it is obvious that many have thought in order not to believe. But not all by any means. Indeed, there are so many variations moving under the banner of Enlightenment that it is necessary to talk about the Enlightenment traditions. Henry F. May casts important light on the Enlightenment when he elaborates the ways in which Enlightenment thought was synthesized with Reformation Christianity in the American founding. More recently, Alasdair MacIntyre has lifted up the importance of the Scottish Enlightenment as a tradition of reason distinctly different from the rationalism associated with other streams of the Enlightenment, especially those most hostile to religion.

But, for all the variety, especially in the understanding of reason and religion, there was something that could be described as "the Enlightenment project." MacIntyre defines it this way: "It was the shared belief of the protagonists of the Enlightenment, whether in its French, its Scottish, or its German versions, that one and the same set of standards of truth and rationality—indeed of right conduct and adequate aesthetic judgment—was not only available to all human beings qua rational persons, but [these standards] were such that no human being qua rational person could deny their authority. The central project of the Enlightenment was to formulate and to apply those standards."

Today's loss of confidence that there are such standards that must be recognized by all rational beings, qua rational beings, has led to what is described as the collapse of the Enlightenment project. Our purpose here is to examine some of the turns taken as a result of that collapse. All of which brings us back to irony, and, more specifically, to the "ironic liberalism" proposed by the late Richard Rorty. Rorty, who was born in 1931 and died in 2007, had a long and distinguished academic career at Princeton, the University of Virginia, and Stanford. He was in his lifetime wreathed with honors. Working through the modes of analytic philosophy that dominate most philosophy departments today, Rorty moved on and declared himself a pragmatist in the lineage of John Dewey, and later abandoned academic philosophy in favor of literary criticism and the humanities more generally, where, he believed, the more interesting questions are explored more interestingly.

Rorty's powerfully argued 1979 book, *Philosophy and the Mirror of Nature,* reflected his definitive break with the tradition of Enlightenment rationalism described by MacIntyre. There were many more books to come, including *Achieving Our Country.* Endowed with an ease of manner and literary grace, Rorty represented for innumerable contemporaries a way of living successfully in the contemporary world by not taking it, or oneself, so very seriously. C. S. Lewis wrote in *The Abolition of Man* that to see through everything is to see nothing, and Rorty proposed that, for the "liberal ironist," there is life, and indeed a reasonably satisfactory life, after nothing.

Rorty's proposal is set forth most provocatively and in greatest detail in his 1989 book, *Contingency, Irony, and Solidarity.* Rorty agrees with MacIntyre's understanding of what the Enlightenment project was about, and, like MacIntyre, he thinks it came to an end quite some time ago. As to what will succeed that project, he comes to conclusions that could hardly be more unlike MacIntyre's, especially with respect to religion. Liberal ironists, says Rorty, know that the Enlightenment project is dead, and what is most dead about it is the rationalist notion that there is reality "out there" that is intellectually apprehensible and that can provide certain knowledge about how the world is and what we ought to do about it. Liberal ironists know, Rorty writes, that there is no universally valid answer to moral questions such as, "Why not be cruel?" "Anybody who thinks that there are well-grounded theoretical answers to this sort of question," writes Rorty, "is still, in his heart, a theologian or a metaphysician. He believes in an order beyond time and change which both determines the point of human existence and establishes a hierarchy of responsibilities."

Not so with liberal ironists, who, Rorty recognizes, are in a distinct minority; or at least those who define themselves as such are in a distinct minority. While the ironic posture is pervasive in our culture, relatively few have thought through its full implications: "The ironist intellectuals who do not believe that there is such an order are far outnumbered . . . by people who believe that there *must* be one. Most non-intellectuals are still committed either to some form of religious faith or to some form of Enlightenment rationalism." In Rorty's view, Enlightenment rationalism is not so much the enemy of religion as another form of religion; both the religious and the rationalists are, as he says, theologians or metaphysicians at heart, and there is hardly a dime's worth of difference between them.

Rorty sums up the intellectual succession in our civilization's story to date by saying that "once upon a time" people felt the need to worship something beyond the visible world. "God," for example. Beginning in the seventeenth century, "we" tried to substitute a love of truth for a love of God, treating the world described by science as a quasi-divinity. That is the phase most commonly associated with the Enlightenment project. Then, beginning at the end of the eighteenth century, came Romanticism, in which "we" tried to replace a love for scientific truth with a love for ourselves, for a worship of our own deep spiritual or poetic nature, treated as one more quasi-divinity. Now, Rorty suggests, comes the time to grow up, to *really* grow up. The liberal ironist wants "to get to the point where we no longer worship *anything*, where we treat *nothing* as a quasi-divinity, where we treat *everything*—our language, our conscience, our community—as a product of time and chance. To reach this point would be, in Freud's words, to 'treat chance as worthy of determining our fate.'"

Set aside for the moment the occasions in which Rorty gets his political wind up and, as in *Achieving Our Country*, portrays liberal democracy as a quasi-religion. Recall his words quoted earlier, "Whitman and Dewey gave us all the romance, and all the spiritual uplift we Americans need to go about our public business." If Rorty is not ironic about the version of liberal democracy that he favors, it is because it is a way of ordering society that permits him and others of like mind to be ironic about everything else. The quasi-religion of liberalism makes possible the *a-religious* worship of nothing.

Whether human beings are capable of worshipping nothing is very much open to doubt. Put differently, one may ask whether worshipping nothing is not, in fact, *worshipping* nothing. Or, yet again, the worship of nothing may in fact be the worship of the self and of what the self does in the face of nothing. It seems quite possible that Rorty is more in the Romantic mode than he suspects. In reading Rorty, one is reminded of the words of the Curé de Torcy in Georges Bernanos' *Diary of a Country Priest.* He is describing the intellectually aspiring young people in his first parish: "They were forever trying to discover what they really were, you could feel them overflowing with sheer self-appreciation." Yet Rorty would certainly object, saying that he is not like those young people at all. With Nietzsche, he discards their "spirit of seriousness" about how the world really is and who they really are. He wants to fuse the aesthetic and the moral, to indulge what Friedrich Schiller called "play," to encourage a deliberate "light-mindedness" about existence.

In an earlier essay, "The Priority of Democracy to Philosophy," Rorty urges us to surrender the notion that there are general ideas pertinent to a just polity. Asking about foundations, justifications, and moral rationales is just a bad habit that we should get over. And we can get over the habit simply by not asking those questions anymore. When others pose such questions, just say no. "To take this view," writes Rorty, "is of a piece with dropping the idea that a single moral vocabulary and a single set of moral beliefs are appropriate for every human community everywhere, and to grant that historical developments may lead us to simply *drop* questions and the vocabulary in which those questions are posed."

It is true that we will still encounter troublesome people who continue to ask those questions in public, failing to recognize that they are, at most, of interest in the private formation of the self. But our moral commitment to a liberal polity, Rorty says, does not require that we take seriously everything that, for moral reasons, is taken seriously by one's fellow citizens. "It may require just the opposite. It may require trying to josh them out of the habit of taking those topics so seriously. There may be serious reasons for so joshing them." And if such people refuse to be joshed out of their bad philosophical habits, if they disrupt the liberal polity with their questions that have no answers, well, we may just have to declare them mentally maladjusted, exclude them from the public square (gently, if possible), and then get on with the business of democracy in the absence of philosophical justifications.

Those who are joshed by Mr. Rorty might understandably be inclined to josh him back. They might, for instance, point out that he has not broken as cleanly as he thinks with the "way of the mind" associated with the Enlightenment project. In important respects, he seems to agree with the imperative expressed by Descartes: "I thought that it was necessary . . . to reject as absolutely false anything concerning which I was able to entertain the least doubt." Rorty would likely respond, however, that his purpose is not to accept or reject any statements about reality; his project is beyond concerns about truth and falsehood, at least as those words have any *public* meaning.

Defending philosophical realism, Etienne Gilson contended that the great choice in philosophy comes down to some very basic oppositions. "It is necessary to choose between Aristotle and St. Thomas (truth is the conformity of intelligence with what is) and Kant in his logic (truth is the accord of reason with itself). Shall we judge reality as a function of knowledge or knowledge as a function of reality? That is the whole question."

Rorty responds that making such a choice is necessary only for "metaphysicians or theologians." Yet he seems to disguise, perhaps even from himself, that he has made such a choice, although not necessarily between the alternatives as posed by Gilson. He has, for instance, made a choice against the suspicion that modern thought, with its radical turn to the knowing subject, was a fundamentally wrong turn. A thorough historicist, one who is committed to contingency without reserve, might entertain that suspicion, might even be persuaded of its truth. For all his declared skepticism, Rorty does not seem to be skeptical enough to question his location of himself on the continuum of modern thought subsequent to the turn alluded to by Gilson. I am not suggesting that the philosophy of the past 200 years is in fact the result of a fundamentally wrong turn; rather, I am suggesting that a theory of contingency that is prepared to "go all the way" should be able to entertain that possibility.

Rorty's course of radical skepticism rejects all "correspondence theories" of truth, whether the "realist" correspondence of subject and object or the "mentalist" correspondence of intrinsically coherent thought. He claims we can say nothing about "reality," about what is "out there"—or at least nothing to which it is appropriate to attach terms such as "true" or "false" in intersubjective (public) discourse. One may be tempted to dismiss that claim as no more than a form of the nihilism familiar since Nietzsche, or, at a less elevated level, as yet another turn on sophomoric solipsism. In that case, one might say with Gilson that serious philosophy has enough problems of its own to resolve without "becoming lost in labyrinths that nobody need enter." But if, with MacIntyre, we understand the history of thought to be one of contesting traditions, it is necessary to know something about the tradition of which Rorty is part. Carefully trailing behind us a strong cord, so that we will be able to find our way back, it is worth entering Rorty's labyrinth to at least have a look around. If I am right in thinking that Rorty has more thoroughly thought through the implications of an "age of irony" than many who think they are following his example, it should be a rewarding exercise, both for those who have studied Rorty and for those who have never heard of him before.

To anyone who shares Rorty's devotion to liberal democracy, *Contingency, Irony, and Solidarity* has a number of appeals. Rorty's "liberal ironist" seems to be a modest fellow who leaves a lot of intellectual space open for things about which we cannot know for sure. He appears to be an easygoing person who does not take himself too seriously, who demonstrates a lively sense of serendipity, and who is prepared to be infinitely tolerant of other people who are more or less like himself, which is to say other people at home in the genteel ambiance of the liberal academy. That may make the liberal ironist sound like a rather parochial figure, but, if so, it is a more pleasant parochialism than some of its alternatives. Rorty insists that he is a pragmatist in the tradition of John Dewey. Unlike Dewey, however, he does not preach "a common faith" necessary to sustaining liberal democracy. To the contrary, in a "light-minded" way that he takes to be a virtue, he proposes that we get along without any faith at all and then "see how things go." That is, it must be admitted, a kind of pragmatism.

Rorty argues that we all carry about a set of words that we use to justify the things that matter most to us. They are the words we use to tell the story of our lives, and Rorty calls them a person's "final vocabulary." They are final in the sense that they are the best we can manage at the moment; we can't go beyond them without falling into helpless passivity or resorting to force. The irony he commends satisfies three criteria.

First, the liberal ironist has radical and continuing doubts about the final vocabulary he currently uses, because he has been impressed by other vocabularies, vocabularies taken as final by people or books he has encountered. Second, he realizes that arguments phrased in his present vocabulary can neither underwrite nor dissolve these doubts. And third, insofar as he philosophizes about his situation, he does not think that his vocabulary is closer to reality than others, that it is in touch with a power not himself. Ironists who are inclined to philosophize see the choice between vocabularies as made neither within a neutral and universal "metavocabulary" nor by an attempt to fight one's way past appearances to the "real," but simply as a matter of playing thc new off against the old.

These three characteristics of ironism are central to Rorty's proposal. The first two, however, are hardly distinctive to the position he would advance. Indeed, radical and continuing doubt about one's own "social construction of reality" because of one's encounter with other such constructions can well be accommodated within many conceptual schemes, including religious traditions. Although, to be sure, in such traditions radical and continuing doubt is not necessarily considered a virtue, except in the limited sense of the persistent "interrogation" discussed by Abelard and mentioned earlier. Similarly, in such traditions it is readily agreed that such doubts cannot be definitively dissolved under existing circumstances, including the circumstance of our personal "final vocabulary."

This situation is usually described in Christian terms as walking by faith and not by sight (2 Cor. 5:7). If "faith" is understood as trust rather than as a way of knowing, and if "sight" means the dissolution of all possible doubt, it would seem that Rorty's ironist equally walks by faith and not by sight. His third criterion is more distinctive by virtue of its (metaphysical?) assumption that one is not in touch with a power that is not oneself, and by its grounding in a dialectic between old and new. At the same time, the third criterion also loses much of its distinctiveness *if* the ironist realizes that his vocabulary has no greater hold on reality *in any philosophically provable sense.* With that amendment (and there would seem to be no reason Rorty should disallow the amendment), the post-Enlightenment Christian can satisfy all three criteria for being an ironist. *If* a post-Enlightenment Christian wants to be an ironist.

Rorty says an ironist is a historicist "all the way down." It is in the utter contingency of language that whatever truth there is *is made by us.* In his Nietzschean history of culture, and in the philosophy of language he embraces, we "see language as we now see evolution, as new forms of life constantly killing off old forms—not to accomplish a higher purpose, but blindly." Language is not a "mirror of nature," it is not a medium between ourselves and reality—whether reality "out there" or reality "deep within ourselves." There are no ahistorical, permanent, highest-level realities that can adjudicate lower-level conflicts. The traditional question is, "How do you know that?" But, says Rorty, about the most important things we can only ask, "Why do you talk that way?"

If we are ironists, says Rorty, we talk as we do so that we, with Nietzsche, will be able to say of our lives, "Thus I willed it!" The traditional use of language is to "express something that was already there," whereas it is our attempt to use language so as "to make something that never had been dreamed of before." The great fear is the fear of not being novel. We fear that our life's project will be lost or forgotten, but we fear much more that, even if our works are remembered, "nobody will find anything distinctive in them." The tragedy is that "one will not have impressed one's mark on the language but, rather, will have spent one's life shoving about already coined pieces."

Our final language, if we live a successful life, proves our liberation from our inherited language. In that case "one would havc *demonstrated* that one was not a copy or a replica." Herein lies the superiority of the "strong poet" to the philosopher, and Rorty extends the title of "poet" far beyond those who write verse. Proust, Newton, Darwin, Hegel, Heidegger, Derrida, and others are strong poets who rebelled against death, death being the failure to be novel. The fear of the strong poets "is the fear that one might end one's days in . . . a world one never made, an inherited world."

The inherited philosophical world with which Rorty associates himself began, he suggests, with Hegel. "Instead of constructing philosophical theories and arguing for them," Rorty writes, "he avoided argument by constantly shifting vocabularies, thereby changing the subject." The critical contribution of Hegel is this: "In practice, though not in theory, he dropped the idea of getting at the truth in favor of the idea of making things new." (One may well wonder what Hegel would make of such a claim, but my purpose here is to discuss not Hegel but Rorty.) We are told that the "young Hegel" broke out of the philosophical sequence that runs from Plato through Kant "and began a tradition of ironist philosophy which is continued in Nietzsche, Heidegger, and Derrida." The distinctive thing about these philosopher-poets is that "they define their achievement by their relation to their predecessors rather than by their relation to the truth."

It is nonsense, we are given to understand, to ask about the truth of this theory of ironism. "The last thing the ironist theorist wants or needs," says Rorty, "is a theory of ironism." Indeed, the implication is that he cannot abide such a theory because such theories inevitably make the ironist vulnerable to the traditional questions about truth. "Ironist theory," Rorty writes, "is thus a ladder which is to be thrown away as soon as one has figured out what it was that drove one's predecessors to theorize." If the ironist is to be able to say, "Thus I willed it!" he has to be able to sum up his life "in his own terms." "He is trying to get out from under inherited contingencies and make his own contingencies, get out from under an old final vocabulary and fashion one which will be all his own." He refuses to be judged by "history" or even by the standards that he has created. Rather, says Rorty, "the jùdge the ironist has in mind is himself."

As "strong poetry" succeeds philosophy, so literary criticism, broadly understood, is the most potent form of strong poetry. The ironist, of course, learns from and interacts with the canon of inherited vocabularies. But that, too, is a ladder to be kicked away. "What [the ironist] is looking for is a redescription of that canon which will cause it to lose the power it has over him—to break the spell cast by reading the books which make up that canon." It seems that even the memory of how he came to his final vocabulary is intolerable. Rorty cites Heidegger's observation that "a regard to metaphysics still prevails even in the intention to overcome metaphysics. Therefore our task is to cease all overcoming, and leave metaphysics to itself."

Heidegger feared that someone would one day do what in fact Derrida has done: treat Heidegger as Heidegger treated Nietzsche, as, in Rorty's words, "one more (the last) rung in a ladder which must be cast away." Although Rorty does not quite put it this way, his purpose—the drive to self-creation by the achievement of utter novelty, the urge to be one's own judge, the struggle for liberation from inherited vocabularies—is closely associated with sterility and death. It follows that successors are the enemy. Children entangle us with others, compromising our singularity. They are hostages to the future, thereby binding us to a future from which we would be free; and they are potential judges, thereby compromising our judgment of ourselves on our own terms.

Rorty quotes Derrida's correspondence with one whom Derrida called his "sweet love." Derrida writes that "what has betrayed us is that you wanted generality, which is what I call a child." Children are like universal public truths or privileged descriptions that "metaphysicians" hope to hand on to posterity in the hope of fending off death and finitude. Derrida says children are just the opposite, however; they tend to patricide and matricide. As the ladders of the past must be kicked away, so also with the ladders from ourselves to the future. They, too, must be kicked away, for they compromise the uniqueness of the life that would say of itself, "Thus I willed it!" Derrida writes to his friend, "At least help me so that death comes to us only from us. Do not give in to generality."

These, then, are some of the things to be seen in Rorty's labyrinth of Enlightenment irony. It is an intriguing place, rich in intellectual displays and learned excuses, frequently concerned, I expect Rorty would agree, more with being playful than with being plausible. He would no doubt quickly add, however, that what most people call "plausible" bears the baggage of inherited vocabularies fatally premised on the notion that language is somehow the medium of "mirroring" how things really are. But now it is time to take the cord we had trailed behind us and find our way back out of the labyrinth, where we might better consider what we have seen and why it so appeals to many intelligent people of our time.

It has been observed that "realism" is more a boast than a school of thought, but Rorty and those of an opposing view, such as Gilson, know that is not right. Realism, or what Rorty disparagingly calls "commonsense," assumes that, yes, language is in some important sense a medium between subject and object, between the mind and what is "out there" or "abidingly deep down within us," even if such a correspondence is not provable beyond possible doubt. Such correspondence, one might suggest, is a "justifiable belief," if not provably "true," a distinction that finds no place in Rorty's language. Justifiable beliefs need not rest on other and more certain beliefs, such as those supported by the sense data demanded by the Enlightenment empiricist, or the product of reason as defined by the rationalist.

Realism, rightly understood, rejects the radical "turn to the subject" that Rorty associates with the Kantian stage of the Enlightenment, as it also rejects Rorty's putative overcoming of the subject/object distinction. Such realism is inescapably "foundationalist," at least in the sense that it operates with some version of a connection between inward and outward reality. Realists of the world unite behind Dr. Samuel Johnson's (nonfoundational!) refutation of Bishop George Berkeley's presumably irrefutable theory about the nonexistence of matter when the good doctor kicked a stone and declared, "I refute it *thus.*" For those who are satisfied with that refutation, there is perhaps no reason to bother with Richard Rorty at all, except, as one might have occasion, to try to josh him out of his views or, as he repeatedly recommends in dealing with the "metaphysicians," to try to "change the subject."

But, given the current intellectual climate, attention must be paid, and attending to Richard Rorty can be good, clean cerebral exercise. For those with a taste for pointing out contradictions and inconsistencies, Rorty also offers rich fare. But they should be forewarned that Rorty has anticipated their attacks on "self-referential inconsistency" by disclaiming any interest in what he dismisses as the logics of consistency, which are inescapably "theological or metaphysical."

Being much closer to the second, Romantic stage of the Enlightenment than he seems to think, Rorty, in effect, says with Whitman, "Do I contradict myself? Very well then I contradict myself (I am large, I contain multitudes)." The varieties in the contingent multitudes, from Plato to Derrida, that have contributed to Rorty's final vocabulary need not be reconciled, for the ladder has been kicked away and we have only to do with the refinement of contingencies that is Richard Rorty, that is, *this self himself.* Charges of inconsistency or moral relativism do not apply to the fulfilled ironist, who does not acknowledge the referents by which inconsistency or relativism might be defined.

The end product is in some respects quite attractive. Rorty and his fellow liberal ironists have many sensible views about "a self-identity which suits one for citizenship in an ideally liberal state." Liberal ironists "combine commitment with a sense of the contingency of their own commitment." The reasons for their commitment to liberal democracy are unexceptionable (dare one say commonsensical?), appealing in a self-interested way to its advantages over alternative arrangements. Against political ideologues on the left and the right, they have a keen sense of the importance of the distinction between private and public, insisting upon a large space for the former and a small space for the latter.

Rorty says he has no use for salvational politics of any sort. Salvation, if it is to be found, is to be found apart from the public arena, in the private sphere of fantasy and experiment, and aimed at self-creation. (As mentioned earlier, this is hard to square with his call for salvational politics in *Achieving Our Country,* unless one understands it to be in the service of private self-creation, which some might view as a form of anti-politics.) There is no doubt about Rorty's devotion to the *liberal* in liberal ironism. He sharply criticizes ironists who are not liberal, Michel Foucault for instance; and he also criticizes liberals who are not ironists, such as Jürgen Habermas. Although he acknowledges that it is small now, he wants to multiply the tribe of those who share his preference for a liberal democracy in which ironic existence is protected from liberal metaphysicians and liberalism is protected from illiberal nihilists.

It must be admitted, however, that the satisfactions in attending to Richard Rorty are reduced by the frequent dogmatism and apodicticism with which he asserts "truths" that are neither argued for nor accommodated by what appears to be his theory of truth. For all his radical skepticism, Rorty appears to "know" an astonishing number of truths—public truths, the kinds of things that his despised "metaphysicians" call facts. On many questions, and by his own account, it seems that science does "discover" truths about things "out there," and is not simply engaged in language games and interesting shifts in habits of discourse.

For instance, Rorty knows that the contributions of such as Aristotle, Saint Paul, Newton, and Bach were the absolutely contingent "results of cosmic rays scrambling the fine structure of some crucial neurons in their respective brains," or of obsessional kinks left in these brains by childhood traumas. Such assertions would seem to be linguistic representations of reality, the very use of language that Rorty says he rejects. The force of his saying that language is a tool for dealing with the world, rather than a representation of the world, is also considerably reduced by his implicit acknowledgment that the tool only works if it has some implicit connection with the way the world is. Yet he refuses to acknowledge that explicitly, because to do so is to open the door to the "metaphysicians or theologians" who believe that philosophy and science have "a priestly function" in mediating "fact" or "objectivity" and thus "putting us in touch with a realm which transcends the human."

Rorty knows so many things that, despite himself, are stated as fact and from which he "logically" (usually a derogatory term in his vocabulary) draws conclusions. He knows what people do and do not fear, he knows that Sigmund Freud has given us a way to understand human behavior that is more adequate than earlier descriptions, he knows the course of history is toward maximizing freedom, and he claims to know that, if we attend to freedom, then goodness and truth will take care of themselves. He even knows that "scientific discoveries" have discredited belief in an immortal soul. The ironist's final vocabulary turns out to be not so formal as it appears; it is filled with contents that other people call facts, and about which, contra the first article of his ironist's creed, Rorty gives no indication of having "radical and continuing doubts."

Rorty writes, "The difference between a search for foundations and an attempt at redescription is emblematic of the difference between the culture of liberalism and older forms of cultural life. For in its ideal form, the culture of liberalism would be one which was enlightened, secular, through and through." That is the ironist's taken-for-granted "construction of reality." Rorty is at points prepared to justify that construction by the declaration, "Thus I willed it!" but at the same time he argues for it by producing evidence from a presumably nonexistent basis in fact. Rorty, despite having declared his immunity to the charge of self-referential inconsistency, might take umbrage at that criticism.

His argument might be somewhat more persuasive if he did not rely so heavily upon caricatures of opposing views. Like Peter Gay claiming that the Enlightenment replaced religion with reason, Rorty depicts pre-ironist Enlightenment figures as people in need of assured certitudes, smugly satisfied that they could logically solve all problems, deluded in their addiction to general theories for explaining reality, and so forth. With respect to the religious versions of this smugness, Rorty seems to be innocent of any acquaintance with religion that is not foundationalist in the sense that he caricatures religion to be, and that is therefore not subject to the criticism he directs at Enlightenment rationalism.

Most dismissively treated is what he assumes is the necessary connection between religion and uncritical certitude. In thinking about the prospects for the human future, ironists have little patience with "the scenario which their grandparents wrote around the turn of the century." One is mindful that one of Rorty's grandparents was Walter Rauschenbusch, the first among the apostles of the Social Gospel movement around the turn of the century. Rorty rejects that movement's putative religious certitudes, but he also declares himself a utopian and at critical points evidences an equally optimistic view of what others call human nature.

Rorty's is a peculiar understanding of religion inherited from the era of liberal rationalistic Protestantism. He assumes religion is incompatible with "commitment to contingent commitment." The religion he has in mind, unlike postliberal Christianity, has everything to do with certitude, and little or nothing to do with faith and hope. He does not address the possibility that even Martin Luther's "Here I stand" qualifies as contingent commitment in that Luther declares himself prepared to recant if convinced by Scripture or clear reason. The difference between Luther's commitment and that of Rorty's ironist is not a difference of certitude but the difference between "Thus I willed it" and "So it is willed."

There is in Rorty what might be described as an egoistic eschatology, and his caricature of religion prevents him from entertaining an alternative eschatology. He says that we can only understand history, including philosophy, in retrospect, from the end toward which it is developing. He says that those who achieved earlier redescriptions could not know what they were doing, "but *we* now know these things, for we latecomers can tell the kind of story of progress which those who are actually making progress cannot. . . . The product is *us*—our conscience, our culture, our form of life."

Compared with, say, the coming of the Kingdom of God, Rorty's ironic achievement is a safely foreshortened End Time. In Rorty's eschatology, it seems that our time is the End Time *because* it is our time. In his way of talking, the uncertainty of radical contingency is blunted by the security that we, here and now, know what history has been about until now. The radical mode of contingent existence that Rorty prizes would seem to be much heightened by a Christian eschatology that, unlike Rorty's, is falsifiable (after all, it is hypothetically conceivable that Jesus will *not* return in glory). Here and elsewhere, Rorty's caricatured dismissals of alternative descriptions of reality are useful only in sustaining his belief in the singularity of the description and consequent mode of existence that he favors. Or, more precisely, the description and mode of existence that he believes he *is*.

His disdain for the metaphysicians of fact notwithstanding, Rorty persistently appeals, as we have seen, to what most would call "facts" in order to buttress his argument. This is the more troubling when he gets his facts thoroughly wrong. A few examples will serve. "The French Revolution," he writes, "had shown that the whole vocabulary of social relations, and the whole spectrum of social institutions, could be replaced almost overnight." At another point he argues at some length that the past 200 years have demonstrated the ability to maintain humane society without reference to religion or belief in accountability to some self-transcending law. Or consider his claim that altruistic behavior—he cites those Gentiles who rescued Jews under Nazism—is occasioned by feelings of "solidarity" with those who share our social situation, rather than by obedience to rules dependent upon general theories. These are but three instances of Rorty's claiming to know what his argument says cannot be known, and in all three instances what he claims to know is, not to put too fine a point on it, simply contrary to fact (if one may be permitted the term).

Simon Schama is among historians of the period who have shown that the French Revolution demonstrated precisely the opposite of what Rorty claims, namely, the perdurance of human behaviors and beliefs that can only be defied with awesomely bloody consequences. The effort to replace them "overnight" produced the Great Terror with death and suffering beyond measure. As for Rorty's assumed secularization, at least American democracy has been accompanied by a continuing, and probably increasing, sense of dependence upon general moral rules, typically grounded in religious belief. Moreover, a massive study of rescuers during the Nazi era demonstrated that the overwhelming majority of them, in explaining their actions, employed the "final vocabularies" of particular communal traditions bearing universal laws and usually expressed in religious terms. Among the hundreds of rescuers studied, there would seem to be none who might qualify as a "liberal ironist." If one is in desperate need of a neighbor's self-sacrificial help, it would seem to be advisable not to have neighbors who are liberal ironists. Here, as elsewhere, the conclusion is reinforced that the kind of society Rorty desires can be neither generated nor sustained on the basis of the philosophy that he espouses.

One cannot help but be impressed by how, in these and other instances, Rorty is so thoroughly mistaken in describing the world of which he is part. But the question might be asked whether it makes much difference to his argument. One answer is that he certainly seems to think it makes a difference, or else he would not have gone to the trouble of marshaling so much (contrary-to-fact) evidence in order to buttress his case. At the very least, his errors undermine the insouciance with which he recommends his thoroughly secular ironic liberalism. The outlook for a society based on ironic liberalism is, one might conclude, very grim indeed.

Admittedly, a societal need for belief in general moral foundations does not mean that such foundations actually exist. But without such belief the prospects for a humane social order would seem to be depressingly dim. Rorty at points comes close to admitting as much, indicating that his community of ironic liberals may always be an enlightened minority dependent upon the "metaphysicians and theologians" whose influence holds the society together. If this is what he really believes, it may be that his complacent proposal for a society based on liberal ironism is but another instance of the "playful" Mr. Rorty not being entirely serious. Or perhaps he is simply reluctant to say right out that his liberal ironism is parasitical, dependent upon other people who sustain society with beliefs—and a readiness to act on beliefs—that the ironist does not share.

The relentless focus on self-creation in *Contingency, Irony, and Solidarity,* Rorty well knows, could be turned to purposes destructive of the democratic solidarity that he affirms. The right way to read his "jargon," he says, is "to think of philosophy as *in the service* of democratic politics." This, as we have seen, requires the sharpest possible distinction between public and private as well as a determination to restrict the sphere of the former and expand the sphere of the latter. In the public sphere there is only one rule that he insists upon: Do not be cruel. But this does not produce an argument, in the sense of foundational reasons, for liberal democracy: "The ironist takes the words which are fundamental to metaphysics, and in particular to the public rhetoric of the liberal democracies, as just another text, just another set of little human things."

The person engaged in the literary critical life will, in his "deconstructing" or "recontextualizing" of texts (Rorty suggests the two are much the same thing), come to "a heightened awareness of the possibility of suffering," but it "will not produce a *reason to care* about suffering." The liberal ironist is not cruel for the simplest of all utilitarian reasons: his hope that other people, in turn, will not be cruel to him. Rorty writes that "human solidarity is not a matter of sharing a common truth or a common goal but of sharing a common selfish hope, the hope that one's world—the little things around which one has woven one's final vocabulary—will not be destroyed."

Although it would seem to be incompatible with his ironist position, Rorty does speak at times about common public purposes by which people are united. At other points, he contends that the vocabulary of giving justifying reasons "was essential to the beginnings of liberal democracy," but such a vocabulary has now "become an impediment to the preservation and progress of democratic societies." "I have been urging," he writes, "that the democracies are now in a position to throw away some of the ladders used in their own construction." Yet at another place he writes, "I cannot go on to claim that there could or ought to be a culture whose public rhetoric is ironist."

It is not entirely easy to understand Rorty at this point. He seems to reject the assumption that intellectuals will be ironists while the masses will always require justifying reasons to behave. Implying that the attitudes of intellectuals can be popularized, he notes that "once upon a time atheism, too, was the exclusive property of intellectuals." (Remember that the liberal democracy of his experience is, for all practical purposes, pervasively atheistic.) However, he then goes on to say, "In the ideal liberal society, the intellectuals would still be ironists, although the non-intellectuals would not." If we did not know that the idea of consistency has been banished, we might be puzzled, but that, as the ironist light-mindedly observes, is our problem, not his.

Abstractions such as "child of God" or "humanity" or "rational being" and "truth for its own sake" are still in the public vocabulary, and Rorty admits that they may have done some good in the past. The problem arises when we think that these "handy bits of rhetoric" are fit subjects for "conceptual analysis." We then discover that they are no more than fuzzy and inspiring *foci imaginarii,* although, he seems to suggest, they may be "useful lies" (Nietzsche) in a culture where most people have not arrived at liberal ironism. So it would seem that, in any society Rorty can imagine or desire, public rhetoric would not be ironist, that irony can only thrive in a non-ironist public culture. This, despite some statements suggesting otherwise, would seem to be Rorty's final position, or at least as far as he got.

There is a sentence in passing that, when one considers its ramifications, would appear to deserve more than a sentence in passing. "I cannot imagine a culture," he writes, "which socialized its youth in such a way as to make them continually dubious about their own process of socialization." One wonders at what point parents and teachers would tell children that what they told them was true is not true in the sense that they intended them to understand that it was true. Upon reflection, no good age for doing so readily suggests itself.

True, many children are told that there is a Santa Claus and, later, are told that there is not. Most seem to take it in stride as part of growing up. But nobody suggests that the social order depends on belief in Santa Claus, whereas Rorty agrees that it depends on belief in right and wrong, in good and evil, and, most important, in the commandment not to be cruel. He cannot imagine a culture that socialized its youth to be continually dubious about such beliefs. As with Gibbon's description of the philosophers of Rome, the credulity of the masses is not only useful but essential to the security of the liberal ironist. There is an element of candor in recognizing that the security of unbelief depends on belief, but one wonders if it is wise in that circumstance to evangelize for unbelief, which is what Rorty certainly does. One wonders whether on these questions it might not be more prudent to write in an "esoteric" mode for the cognoscenti. One wonders, finally, if Mr. Rorty is serious about all this. Of course, he might be serious if, as he sometimes suggests, the ironist is, like Derrida, indifferent or even hostile to the idea of a successor generation. That would seem to follow from an eschatology that has no horizon beyond the self.

Rorty says that irony is a purely private matter, and yet by an ironist philosophy he would serve the manifestly public cause of liberal democracy. Thus he implicitly acknowledges that those things we care about deeply have a public and societal dimension. Presumably he had in his own life more intimate relationships, which are also social, about which he did not nurture "radical and continuing doubts." But perhaps not. On his view, nothing approximating unconditional love is possible. Nothing is loved for itself except the self; there is no good beyond the self, never mind a *summum bonum.* All is instrumental to self-creation. A self that has only instrumental relations to other selves would seem, however, to be a pitiably shriveled self.

There is no doubt about Rorty's desire to preserve and strengthen a humane social order. In a later essay, "Solidarity or Objectivity," he contends that "Rawlsian searchers for consensus, the heirs of Socrates, the people who wish to link their days dialectically each to each," must learn to value "some" of the institutions of liberalism while refusing to accept the philosophical premises of those institutions. But that, one observes, is no more than an expression of wistful hope that some useful institutions and practices might be rescued from the philosophical rubble.

Further, while he seems to know that even the "self" is itself socially constructed, Rorty's project of self-creation is aimed at denying or overcoming what he knows. Put differently, the project is one of overcoming the self, including what has gone into the making of the self, which leaves, precisely, nothing. And that returns us to the question at the start as to whether, when one's ultimate concern is nothing—when one worships nothing—then one *worships* nothing. Since even the most original self is but the more-or-less novel reconfiguration of inherited vocabularies, the overcoming of that self, or so it seems, must finally mean the destruction of that self.

Thus the suspicion is strengthened that Derrida's embrace of sterility and death is not an aberration but the logical end of the ironist project. To recognize that, and therefore to be ready to let go of the ironist project itself, is perhaps the perfect illustration of acting upon Freud's counsel "to treat chance as worthy of determining our fate." Of course the ironist who follows the project through to that end is ever aware of the (ironic) truth that that is the chance he has *chosen,* and therefore it may not be chance, in the ordinary sense of the term, at all.

Rorty's reversion to "fate," as a neutral metavocabulary by which to view possible vocabularies, begs the question. He has made a choice; and the choice between what he describes as "fighting one's way past appearances to the real," on the one hand, or "playing the new off against the old," on the other, is not philosophically decidable. One has at least equally good grounds for choosing the one as the other. His choice for the dialectic between new and old follows from prior choices. The question to Rorty is, "Why do you *choose* to talk the way you do?" It is not a lack of conversational geniality but his theory that prevents him from answering, except to say, with Nietzsche, "Thus I willed it!"

Then there are more practical considerations (if anything can be more practical than the quest for alternatives to sterility and death). Rorty worries that some ironists, like Nietzsche and Heidegger, are no friends of liberalism or democracy. What is one to do with such people? His answer: "One can ask these men to *privatize* their projects, their attempts at sublimity—to view them as irrelevant to politics and therefore compatible with the sense of human solidarity which the development of democratic institutions has facilitated. This request for privatization amounts to the request that they resolve an impending dilemma by subordinating sublimity to the desire to avoid cruelty and pain. In my view, there is nothing to back up such a request, nor need there be."

There is no indication that Rorty is not entirely serious about this. He leaves no doubt that he knows the kinds of politics that are heir to such as Nietzsche and Heidegger. Confronted by Stalin who plans to do some nasty things to the kulaks, or Hitler who has similar designs on the Jews, Rorty would request that they "privatize" their projects in order to avoid cruelty and pain. Or, as he puts it elsewhere, he would try to josh them out of their crazy ideas. Failing that, he would play his trump card and "change the subject." We might well wish him luck. One is inclined to hope that, confronted by history's more aggressive nonliberal ironists, our request that they cease and desist will be backed up by good reasons, and a readiness to act on those reasons.

"You may well hope for such good reasons," Rorty might reply, "but the fact is that there are none." That is, so to speak, his bottom line. And that, too, despite his protest, is his "self-referential contradiction," for, like Nietzsche and Derrida and a host of others, he claims to know what he claims cannot be known. He claims to know that there are no good reasons for—among a host of matters pertinent to maintaining a livable world—not being cruel.

Although Rorty's public reasoning against the possibility of public reason is not persuasive, there are, as I have indicated, attractive elements in his thought, notably his (usually) modest view of politics and understanding of the dangers of politicizing the spheres in which final felicities are to be sought. But, his intentions to the contrary, he makes it quite clear that the liberal distinction between public and private cannot be defended on ironist grounds. If there is no alternative to his version of ironism, it would indeed seem that the jig is up for liberal culture.

There are alternative and more attractive final vocabularies for people who are, in Rorty's phrase, "historicists all the way down." We do not need to settle for "simply playing off the new against the old." To settle for that is, finally, no more than an arbitrary choice. To be sure, if one makes that choice, the imperative may then be to "make" the only truth there is by developing a final vocabulary that "dissolves the inherited" and precludes the perceived terror of "getting stuck in one's native language." But, instead of pursuing self-creation by playing the new against the old, one may be persuaded that the best thing to do, even the fullest realization of the self, is identification with existing final vocabularies—vocabularies that are not only "talked" but also lived out in individual lives and communal narratives.

Recognizing the contingency of all vocabularies, one may find in an existing vocabulary such compelling intimations of the good, the beautiful, and, yes, the true that one has no higher desire than to be part of the continuation of that final vocabulary. We may all well live in the house of words, but some houses have words that claim to tell us what really is "out there" and "deep down within," and we have no way of knowing—not with undoubtable certitude, not yet—whether those words are true. Neither does anyone know whether they are false. And, one adds, neither does anyone, including Rorty, know beyond the possibility of doubt whether speaking of truth and falsehood in this way does or does not have any bearing on what is really real.

For many of us, Christianity is such a final vocabulary. The orthodox Christian and, I expect, the observant Jew can readily entertain the possibility of contingency "all the way down," that everything "just happened," including the appearance of the notion that everything just happened. But he is persuaded—he cannot prove but is persuaded by compelling reasons leading to justified beliefs—that in what Rorty calls the historical "upshot" it *will be* proved that everything did not just happen. Of course, the Christian's upshot, unlike Rorty's, does not have to do with an eschatology that terminates in the self. From his caricatures of religion in general and of Christianity in particular, as well as from the literature and arguments he cites as being pertinent to the questions he is addressing, it seems that Mr. Rorty has not seriously (or even "playfully," in the serious sense in which he uses that term) considered the merits of such religion as a final vocabulary.

Aside from the not unpleasant duty of joshing Rorty, spending some time with the "way he talks" helpfully illumines the continuity in a certain Enlightenment tradition. As noted earlier, Rorty believes the ironist project is a third stage of the Enlightenment, succeeding rationalism and Romanticism. But the continuities are also striking. They are evident in the attitudes toward religion, tradition, and authority ("inherited vocabularies"). They are evident in that Rorty's ironist, as much as Descartes or Hume, begins from an individualistic premise of radical and systematic skepticism. And, of course, what he calls the Romanticist stage of the Enlightenment is constitutive of his own project of self creation.

The autonomous hero of uncompromised novelty (or at least as uncompromised as possible, given our entanglement in inherited vocabularies) declares himself to *be* in the face of death and the extinction of meaning. With Nietzsche, Rorty's ironists declare, in his own words: "We would seek consolation, at the moment of death, not in having transcended the animal condition but in being that peculiar sort of dying animal who, by describing himself in his own terms, had created himself." "Thus I willed it!" That is not the entirety of Romanticism, but that is undoubtedly Romanticism.

At the beginning of his project, Rorty says that he cannot, in principle, prove the truth of his vocabulary, and he is not going to offer arguments against vocabularies that he wants to replace. "Instead, I am going to try to make the vocabulary I favor look attractive by showing how it may be used to describe a variety of topics." In other words, he wants to persuade us that his ironist way of talking is a better way of living out our being-in-the-world. But he eschews all referents by which "better" or "worse" might be determined, except the desire to continue liberal democracy, meaning a society of people much like himself who achieve an utterly unique final vocabulary. Thus his project results in, as he puts it, "philosophy in the service of democratic politics."

Since his philosophy is in the service of such politics, it provides no measures by which such politics can be either criticized or affirmed. Of his politics, as of his self, Rorty is saying, in effect, "This is the way it is. Take it or leave it." The reader, then, is left free to choose whether, for private purposes, he wants to talk the way Richard Rorty talks. It is a way that is, in the words of the Cure de Torcy, "overflowing with sheer self-appreciation," and for that reason, among others, it is, for all its charming turns, aesthetically unattractive. As Rorty rightly reminds us, there is a closer connection than is usually thought between the aesthetic and the moral. Rorty has told us why he talks the way he does in the only way that his ironism allows him to tell us, namely, autobiographically. Finally, his only subject is himself, as he would persuade us that our only subject is our selves. He hopes that we will find his talk about himself engaging. It does seem to come down to being a matter of taste. As Rorty in principle cannot remind us, but other vocabularies do remind us, there are also connections between the aesthetic, the moral, and the true. All three enter into one's response to Rorty's effort to so severely limit the subject matter for authentic conversation.

In addition, and despite his subordination of the public to the private, Rorty's final justification for his way of talking is thoroughly public in nature—because it is the best way to sustain the liberal democracy that he, along with most of us, favors. We have had occasion to point out some of the ways in which Rorty's ironist vocabulary fails in precisely that task, for it can neither provide a public language for the citizens of such a democracy, nor contend intellectually against the enemies of democracy, nor transmit the reasons for democracy to the next generation. Rorty's public justification of ironic liberalism thus fails on its own stated terms.

So now we have followed Rorty's advice and asked him, "Why do you talk that way?" We have talked about him and to him in the present tense, as though he is present as a partner in conversation, for he obviously intended to continue speaking through his writings. We have listened carefully to what he has to say, and it is time to follow his advice again; it is time to change the subject.

But not before we note that for Richard Rorty, too, the subject was finally and abruptly changed, and in a manner most unoriginal. Told that he had inoperable pancreatic cancer, he wrote an essay, "Fire of Life," that was published in the November 2007 issue of *Poetry* magazine several months after his death. Rorty had often written that, at the end of a successful life in which one has achieved his "final vocabulary," one would be able to say with Nietzsche, "Thus I willed it!"

But now the subject had changed. In "Fire of Life," the fires of individual self-creation are reduced to embers, if not ashes. He writes that he has been asked whether, in the face of death, he finds anything that he has read to be of any use. Yes, he answers, a few poems that he describes as "old chestnuts." He found himself oddly cheered by the lines of Swinburne's "Garden of Prosperine":

> *We thank with brief thanksgiving*
> *Whatever gods may be*
> *That no life lives for ever;*
> *That dead men rise up never;*
> *That even the weariest river*
> *Winds somewhere safe to sea.*

It is a piece of embarrassingly sentimental doggerel. It is hard to know why that would have been cheering, even "oddly" cheering, unless it is the wan hope that the final vocabulary that is oneself is somehow part of the river that is winding somewhere—somewhere safe, somewhere free at last from used vocabularies. In this most unoriginal hope, he will, perhaps, be protected from unoriginality.

"I would have lived more fully," writes Richard Rorty in that final essay, "if I had been able to rattle off more old chestnuts—just as I would have if I had made more close friends. Cultures with richer vocabularies are more fully human—farther removed from the beasts—than those with poorer ones; individual men and women are more fully human when their memories are amply stocked with verses." A few more verses, a few more close friends. The former were amply available. The making of close friends, one might surmise, is not easy when all relationships are viewed as instrumental to the creation of the final vocabulary that is the liberal ironist's eschatological hope of becoming an unprecedented self.

For all the intelligence and learning, for all the literary grace, for all the personal charm, one must ask whether Mr. Rorty's project is an advance over the ballad of Narcissus made popular by Frank Sinatra so many years ago, "I Did It My Way." Although very different in intellectual style, is his proposal substantively different from the generic title of those shelves upon shelves of self-help books at the local Barnes and Noble, *How to Be the Unique Self That You Are*? One would like to answer in the negative.

And now the ladder is rudely pulled away, the aspiration to uniqueness that was Richard Rorty has departed, and we may pray that the "chance" he chose and so assiduously worked at constructing as his final vocabulary will not define his final destination.

It is possible that some readers may think I have paid altogether too much attention to Richard Rorty. After all, he is dead, and even on that subject he was reduced to what he recognized as banalities. (One is reminded of the headline in the satirical magazine *The Onion* upon the death of Jacques Derrida: "Derrida is 'Dead'"—a fitting headline for Rorty's obituary as well.) By discussing him in such detail, am I not complicit in his project of perpetuating his "final vocabulary"? Or am I guilty of using him as a straw man to score intellectual points? In short, does Richard Rorty matter all that much?

I think the answer is yes. Not only because of his influence in our intellectual culture, but because, with rare relentlessness, he followed through on one possible response to our human circumstance in exile. His is a way of responding to that circumstance: Make it up as you go along; take ironic delight in the truth that there is no truth; there is no home that answers to our homelessness; defiantly (but light-headedly!) throw the final vocabulary that is your life in the face of nothingness. And if your neighbor or some inner curiosity persists in asking about the meaning of it all, simply change the subject. Such is the way of muddling through in an "Age of Irony." Richard Rorty matters because contemporaries beyond numbering, most of whom have never heard of Richard Rorty, are living their lives in the mode of the liberal ironism he depicted with such rare and chilling candor.

VI

Salvation Is from the Jews

I HAVE BEEN suggesting throughout these pages that the alternative to resigning ourselves to exile without end—whether that resignation takes the form of Stoic defiance, utopian dreams of progress, or ironic liberalism—is the narrative of history, and of our lives in history, moving toward the Kingdom of God, and being encountered by the Kingdom of God moving toward us. This is, to be sure, the Christian narrative, but it is the Christian narrative that can only be understood if it is understood as the Jewish narrative. It is not simply that the Christian narrative is derived from or presumes the Jewish narrative, as though the Jewish narrative is merely a presupposition that is superseded and now left behind. The "Old Testament" lives in the "New Testament." The people of the old covenant, the Jewish people who are "Israel according to the flesh," live in the people of the new covenant, and vice versa. When Christians forget this, as they have all too often, we lose our hold on "the story of the world," and of our part in that story.

The Samaritan woman said, "Sir, I perceive that you are a prophet. Our fathers worshipped on this mountain; and you say that in Jerusalem is the place where men ought to worship." Jesus responded, "Woman, believe me, the hour is coming when neither on this mountain nor in Jerusalem will you worship the Father. You worship what you do not know; we worship what we know, for salvation is from the Jews."

That exchange from the Gospel of John is also connected, and connected closely, with our discussion of what it means to live in exile in Babylon. The Jews were there first. When under Cyrus they were allowed to return to Jerusalem, and many centuries later, in 1948, when the state of Israel was established, it did not mean the end of exile. Exile, in the deepest and most enduring sense of that term, continues until the arrival of the Messianic Age, the Kingdom of God, the New Jerusalem. The drama of salvation awaits a final act. Christians and Jews in exile together await the End Time, the Eschaton. It is an active waiting, bearing witness now, in word and deed, to what is to be.

Jesus said, "Salvation is from the Jews." Despite its suggestive power, that striking statement is seldom encountered in the now vast literature on what is called the Jewish-Christian dialogue. There are several possible reasons for this. One is that the exchange with the Samaritan woman is entangled with a dispute about "supersessionism" that is quite distinct from the dispute over whether Christianity has superseded or displaced Judaism. The Samaritans—the *shamerim,* which means "observant"—claimed to be the true Israel who remained loyal to Yahweh in the fourth century B.C. when Eli the priest allegedly seduced his brethren into constructing the shrine at Shiloh instead of at God's chosen mountain, Gerizim.

After that schism, Jews forbade Samaritans to make offerings in Jerusalem, to buy unmovable property, or to marry or circumcise a Jew. John's Gospel puts it bluntly, "Jews have no dealings with Samaritans." Judaism in Jerusalem had definitively superseded the cult of the Samaritans of Gerizim. Thus the exchange with the Samaritan woman at Jacob's well is something of an embarrassment in today's Jewish Christian dialogue, a dialogue that is greatly concerned with the question of supersessionism.

Another reason the conversation at the well receives such little attention may be that much of today's conversation between Christians and Jews deliberately avoids the question of salvation, which is the subject of the exchange between Jesus and the Samaritan woman. Today's Jewish-Christian conversation is most frequently about encouraging intergroup relations, overcoming prejudice, and promoting tolerance, all of which are undoubtedly good and important goals. But, at the deeper level of the Jewish-Christian encounter is the ultimate question of salvation.

Commentators on the exchange at the well sometimes pass over it lightly. For instance, a recent ecumenical Christian commentary on the passage says that Jesus was acknowledging only that "God's salvation to humanity came historically through the Jews as a point of departure, not as origin or source. Salvation comes only from God." "A point of departure"—the phrase has a dismissive ring to it, almost as though Jews and Judaism are, for Christians, a dispensable accident of history.

Rudolf Bultmann, a New Testament scholar of inestimable influence during the twentieth century, has a footnote in his commentary on John in which he gives the passage even shorter shrift. The passage is, he says, "completely or partially an editorial gloss," since the statement that salvation is from the Jews is "impossible in John [who] does not regard the Jews as God's chosen and saved people." "It is hard to see," he writes, "how the Johannine Jesus, who constantly disassociates himself from the Jews, could have made such a statement." This is hardly persuasive. A question that Bultmann does not address is why a later editor, presumably at a time when the lines between Jews and Christians had hardened, would have inserted such a statement. It seems improbable that an editor was trying to rectify what Bultmann views as the anti-Jewish bias of John's Gospel. It is more likely, I think, that Jesus said what he is said to have said, and that Bultmann's view reflects his difficulty, and the difficulty that too many other Christians also have, in coming to terms with the Jewishness of Jesus.

In his 1955 commentary on John, the distinguished C. K. Barrett offers what may be taken as a more conventional supersessionist interpretation of the words of Jesus: "The saying does not mean that Jews as such are inevitably saved, but rather that the election of Israel to a true knowledge of God was in order that, at the time appointed by God, salvation might proceed from Israel to the world, and Israel's own unique privilege be thereby dissolved. . . . This eschatological salvation is in the person of Jesus in process of realization and the Jews are losing their position to the Church."

Saint Augustine, as we might expect, treats the passage more imaginatively. Samaritans were "aliens" to the Jews, he notes, and so it is that the woman at the well represents the Church, which "was to come of the Gentiles, an alien from the race of the Jews." Thus Jesus is saying that the Jewish supersession of the Samaritans is now being reversed by the Church, which is composed of "Samaritan" Gentiles who now supersede the Jews. In a less imaginative vein, Augustine writes, "A great thing has Jesus attributed to the Jews." Then he immediately adds, "But do not understand him to mean those spurious Jews [who rejected the Christ]." Citing Saint Paul in Ephesians 2, he says that Samaritans and Gentiles were "strangers and foreigners" to the covenants of God. When Jesus says, "We worship what we know," he is speaking "in the person of the Jews, but not of all Jews, not of reprobate Jews, but of such as were the apostles, as were the prophets." Augustine cites Romans 9 through 11, the essential text on these questions, and affirms that "God has not rejected his people whom he foreknew." By "his people," however, Augustine means only those Jews who are reconciled with the former aliens, namely, the Gentiles, in Christ and his Church.

Few thinkers have pondered these ideas more deeply than Franz Rosenzweig, a German thinker who died in 1929 and is an unavoidable interlocutor when Jewish-Christian dialogue is prepared to take on the hard questions. Rosenzweig returned to Judaism after a very close brush with becoming a Christian. His thought is frequently, if too simply, summarized in the proposition that Christianity is Judaism for the Gentiles. He did not fudge the fact that both Judaism and Christianity are centrally concerned with salvation, as is evident in the title of his major work, *The Star of Redemption.*

In the tradition of such in-depth dialogue is the historic statement of November 2000, *Dabru Emet* (Speak the Truth). Signed by almost 200 notable Jewish scholars, the statement affirms that "through Christianity hundreds of millions of people have entered into relationship with the God of Israel." The statement also says, "We respect Christianity as a faith that originated within Judaism and that still has significant contacts with it. We do not see it as an extension of Judaism. Only if we cherish our own traditions can we pursue this relationship with integrity."

Yet it would seem that, if through Christianity hundreds of millions of people have entered into relationship with the God of Israel, Christianity must, in some important sense, be an extension of Judaism. Moreover, *Dabru Emet* makes clear that this relationship is one of worshipping "the God of Abraham, Isaac, and Jacob," underscoring that the God of Israel cannot be separated from the people of Israel, the children of Abraham, Isaac, and Jacob. It follows that to be in relationship with the God of Israel is to be in relationship with the people of Israel.

In the documents of the Second Vatican Council, a favored phrase for the Church is "the People of God." *There is no plural for the people of God.* As for the statement in the *Dabru Emet* that Jews must cherish their own traditions if they are to "pursue this relationship with integrity," one could respond that "Certainly there are distinct traditions that must be cherished and respected, but they are traditions within the one tradition, the one story, of salvation." That story of God's dealings with Israel and the Church is nothing less than "the story of the world." One might press the point of there being only one tradition by observing that, after the destruction of the temple in Jerusalem in A.D. 70, there came into being two rival versions of Judaism. When the religious observance centered in the temple was no longer possible, one version became what we have known for almost 2,000 years as rabbinical Judaism. The other, soon to be composed mainly of Gentiles, became the Church.

Contemporary Judaism and contemporary Christianity are two different traditions within the one tradition of witness to the God of Israel and his one plan of salvation. It would be profoundly misleading to speak of two peoples of God, or of two covenants, never mind to speak of two religions. It is not Christian imperialism but fidelity to revealed truth, as Christians understand that truth, that requires Christians to say that Christ is Lord of all or he is not Lord at all. It is significant that, after the Second Vatican Council, when the Catholic Church was formalizing its conversations with non-Christians, the Jewish interlocutors insisted that Jewish relations not be grouped under the Vatican office that deals with other religions, but instead included under the Pontifical Council for Promoting Christian Unity. That arrangement has much deeper implications than were perhaps realized at the time.

The salvation that is from the Jews cannot be proclaimed or lived apart from the Jews. This is not to deny that innumerable Christians, indeed the vast majority of Christians, have lived their Christian faith without much awareness of or contact with Jews. Obviously, they have and they do. The percentage of Christians involved in any form of Jewish-Christian dialogue is minuscule. Minuscule, too, is the percentage of Jews involved. Moreover, serious dialogue is, for the most part, a North American phenomenon. It is one of the many things to which the familiar phrase applies, "Only in America." In Europe, for tragically obvious reasons, there are not enough Jews; in Israel, for reasons of growing tragedy in the decline of ancient communities, there are not enough Christians. Only in America are there enough Jews and Christians in a relationship of mutual security and respect to make possible a dialogue that is unprecedented in our 2,000 years of history together.

The significance of this dialogue, however, is not limited to America. For all the variations within both Judaism and Christianity, there is finally only one people of Israel, as there is only one Church. Providential purpose in history is a troubled subject, and the idea of America's providential purpose is even more troubled, but I think we would not be wrong to believe that this dialogue, so closely linked to the American experience, is an essential part of the unfolding of the "story of the world." We are understandably skeptical when it is claimed that something is historically unprecedented. But sometimes that is the case. Here the words of the prophet Isaiah apply: "Remember not the former things, nor consider the things of old. Behold, I am doing a new thing; now it springs forth, do you not perceive it?"

It is fair to say that neither Christians nor Jews would have seen this new thing or acted upon it were it not for the unspeakable tragedy of the Holocaust. This is recognized in *Dabru Emet,* which says of the Christian understanding of Judaism, "In the decades since the Holocaust, Christianity has changed dramatically." It should also be recognized that Judaism has also changed, if not so dramatically, as is evident in a statement such as *Dabru Emet.* Following World War II, Jewish-Christian "dialogue" was for some years conducted mainly in the accusative mode. In this mode, the chief duty of Christians was to engage in rites of self-denigration for wrongs committed against Jews and Judaism. Strident attacks on Christianity, and on Catholicism in particular, by such as Rolf Hochhuth and his 1964 play *The Deputy,* were not uncommon. Some Jewish organizations and a good many self-deprecating Christians are still trapped in that mode. Nor can it be denied that, without Jews in the role of prosecutor and Christians in the role of defendant, the great change in Jewish-Christian relations would not have come about. As it is said, God writes straight with crooked lines.

Admittedly, there are Jews for whom "Never again!" means never enough of Christian self-denigration. We must try to contain our impatience, recognizing the burden of historical grievances and suspicions as well as the institutional interest of some organizations in exploiting them. But there are signs that the dialogue is becoming more truly a dialogue. Indeed it may be said that, through the convoluted ways of history, we are at last catching up with the 1920s' dialogue between Rosenzweig and his friend, the Christian Eugen Rosenstock Huessy, which was emphatically a dialogue about salvation—the salvation that comes from the Jews. Authentic dialogue is a dialogue between friends, and it is not always possible to say which comes first, dialogue or friendship.

Still today there are Jews who resist a dialogue about salvation because that is necessarily a theological dialogue, and they do not want Christians to make Judaism a part of the Christian story. Similarly, there may be Christians who resent efforts such as *Dabru Emet* that tend to make Christianity part of the Jewish story. Advancing the dialogue requires, I believe, our recognition that the Christian story and the Jewish story are only of theological interest as they participate in the story of the one God of Israel. Along the way there are many stories, but ultimately the story of salvation, like the phrase "the people of God," has no plural.

Today it is commonly said that Christianity needs to reappropriate its Jewish dimensions, including the Jewishness of Jesus, and that is undoubtedly part of the truth. But this should not be understood as a matter of taking some parts from the Jewish house next door in order to renovate our Christian house. We live in the same house, of which Christians say with Saint Paul that the Jewish Christ is the cornerstone. To change the metaphor somewhat, we live in the house of the one people of God only as we live with the Jews, and Jesus was—and eternally is—a Jew. The second person of the Holy Trinity, true God and true man, is of Jewish flesh received from the Jewish virgin—as is the eucharistic body we receive, and the Body of Christ into which we are incorporated by baptism. It is said that when John XXIII, then papal nuncio in Paris, first saw the pictures of the piles of corpses at Auschwitz, he exclaimed, "There is the Body of Christ!"

All such insights are but variations on the words of Paul, which we must, as Christians, ever keep at the center of our reflections on the mystery of living Judaism. In the Book of Romans, Paul writes: "But if some of the branches were broken off and you, a wild olive shoot, were grafted in their place to share the richness of the olive tree, do not boast over the branches. If you do boast, remember it is not you that support the root, but the root that supports you. . . . So do not be proud, but stand in awe." Paul's words echo those of Jesus at the well: "Salvation is from the Jews." This people is not a "point of departure," but remains until the end of time inseparable from our point of arrival. By the appointment of the one God whom we worship, we travel together, joined in awe of one another, sometimes in fear of one another, always in argument with one another, until that final point of arrival when, as Paul says to the Corinthians, "we shall know even as we are known."

When we Christians do not walk together with Jews, we are in danger of regressing to the paganism from which we emerged. Rosenzweig saw that gnosticism, pantheism, and the idolatry of culture and nation are constant temptations for Christians. In 1929 he was prescient in foreseeing what would happen in Germany: "The nations have been in a state of inner conflict ever since Christianity with its supernational power came upon them. Ever since then, and everywhere, a Siegfried is at strife with that stranger, the man of the cross (*des gekreuzigten Mannes*), in his very appearance so suspect a character. . . . This stranger who resists the continued attempts to assimilate him to that nation's own self-idealization."

Marcion was a second-century Christian theologian who taught that Judaism and Christianity were two separate religions, indeed that the God of Moses and the God of Jesus were antithetical. He was declared a heretic and excommunicated by the Church of Rome in A.D. 144. But Marcionism is not a one-time heresy. As Rosenzweig recognized, new Marcions are ever at hand to seduce Christianity into becoming a culture-religion, a tribal moralism, or but another spirituality of self-aggrandizement. Christianity does indeed seek to engage culture, provide a guide for living, and propose the way to human flourishing, but, reduced to any of these undoubtedly good ends, it is not Christianity.

Liberal Protestant theology, taking its cue from the Enlightenment, was much preoccupied with the question of "the essence of Christianity," and, not incidentally, was contemptuous of Jews and Judaism. From Immanuel Kant to historians Adolf von Harnack and Arnold Toynbee, Judaism was viewed as an anachronism, a fossil that was destined to wither and die. Christianity, however, is not defined by a moral or metaphysical "essence" but by the man of the cross, a permanently suspect character, forever a stranger of that strange people, the Jews. Through Jesus the Jew, we Christians are anchored in history, defined not by abstract ideas but by a most particular story involving a most particular people.

With respect to Judaism, Christians today are exhorted to reject every form of supersessionism, and so we should. To supersede means to nullify, to void, to make obsolete, to displace. The end of supersessionism, however, cannot and must not mean the end of the argument between Christians and Jews. We cannot settle into the comfortable interreligious politeness of mutual respect for contradictory positions deemed to be equally true. Christ and his Church do not supersede Judaism, but they do continue and fulfill the story of which we are both part. Or so Christians must contend.

It is the story that begins with Abraham, whom we call—in the canon, the central prayer of the Eucharist—"our father in faith." There is no avoiding the much vexed question of whether this means that Jews should enter into the further fulfillment of the salvation story by becoming Christians. Christians cannot, out of a desire to be polite, answer that question in the negative. We can and must say that the ultimate duty of each person is to form his conscience in truth and act upon that discernment; we can and must say, too, that there are great goods to be sought in dialogue apart from conversion, and that we reject proselytizing, which is best defined as evangelizing by demeaning the other. Friendship between Jew and Christian can be secured in our shared love for the God of Israel; the historical forms we call Judaism and Christianity will be transcended, but not superseded, by the fulfillment of eschatological promise. But along the way to that final fulfillment, there is no avoiding the fact that we are locked in argument. It is an argument by which—for both Jew and Christian—conscience is formed, witness is honed, and friendship deepened. This is our destiny, and this is our duty, as members of the one people of God—a people of God for which there is no plural.

At the end of his anguished ponderings in Romans 9:11, having arrived at the farthest reaches of analysis and explanation, the apostle Paul dissolves into doxology: "O the depth of the riches and wisdom and knowledge of God! How unsearchable are his judgments and how inscrutable his ways! . . . For from him and through him and to him are all things. To him be glory forever. Amen."

Along the way to the eschatological resolution of our disagreements, Jews and Christians encourage one another to wait faithfully upon the Lord. Not all Jews and not all Christians agree with this way of understanding the matter. Christopher Leighton, executive director of the Institute for Christian and Jewish Studies, writes that "plurality and difference are the inescapable realities of our existence, and any theological attempt to dissolve our diversity through appeals to a higher truth or a totalizing unity are suspect, even when projected against an eschatological horizon." He goes on to say that "the challenge for Christian theology is to accept, perhaps even celebrate, the gaps, the silences, the distances between us Christians and Jews."

That is in some respects an attractive view, and it should not be dismissed as being no more than interreligious politesse. But it is, I believe, finally inadequate. "Totalizing" is, of course, a pejorative term, but it is precisely a definitive and comprehensive eschatological resolution that we await. Leighton is surely right to say, however, that along the way we should engage the Jewish people "as a mystery in whose company we may discover our own limits and in whose midst we may also discern new and unsuspected insights into ourselves, the world, and God."

It is precisely that spirit of discovery and discernment that marks the Second Vatican Council's "Declaration on the Relationship of the Church to Non-Christian Religions" (*Nostra Aetate*). Note that the declaration was about the Church, not simply about individual or group relations. Here the mystery of the Church encounters the mystery of the Jewish people: "As this sacred Synod searches into the mystery of the Church, it recalls the spiritual bond linking the people of the New Covenant with Abraham's stock." Note that the Church does not go *outside* herself but more deeply *within* herself to engage Jews and Judaism. This is of a piece with Rosenzweig's observation that Christianity becomes something else when it is not centered in the Jewish "man of the cross." *Nostra Aetate* continues: "Nor can [the Church] forget that she draws sustenance from the root of that good olive tree onto which have been grafted the wild olive branches of the Gentiles. Indeed, the Church believes that by His cross Christ, our Peace, reconciled Jew and Gentile, making them both one in Himself (cf. Ephesians 2:14–16)."

Note again that the statement that the Church *draws* sustenance from the Jewish people is in the present tense. It is not simply that she drew sustenance in her beginnings; she now, and perhaps until the end of time, draws sustenance. Also with Muslims and others, *Nostra Aetate* enjoins understanding, respect, study, and dialogue, but only with reference to the Jews does the declaration say that we are dealing with the very mystery of the Church, and therefore the story of salvation. There would be Christianity if Islam and other religions were not. Christianity would not be without Judaism.

At least for Catholics, *Nostra Aetate* marks the beginning of the present Jewish-Christian dialogue. That dialogue has produced many additional documents, official and unofficial, over the years. One may ask whether there have been advances over *Nostra Aetate* in Catholic understanding, and if so, how those advances came about. That question necessarily engages the thought of John Paul II, who, it is universally acknowledged, made unprecedented contributions to Catholic-Jewish relations. In his extended reflection on Jews and Judaism in his remarkable little book, *Crossing the Threshold of Hope,* the pope observes that "the New Covenant has its roots in the Old. The time when the people of the Old Covenant will be able to see themselves as part of the New is, naturally, a question to be left to the Holy Spirit." A purpose of the dialogue, if not *the* purpose of the dialogue, he adds, is "not to put obstacles in the way" of Jews coming to that recognition.

Note that he speaks of when, not whether, this will happen. As though to leave no doubt on this point, he goes on to discuss "how the New Covenant serves to fulfill all that is rooted in the vocation of Abraham, in God's covenant with Israel at Sinai, and in the whole rich heritage of the inspired Prophets who, hundreds of years before that fulfillment, pointed in the Sacred Scriptures to the One whom God would send in the 'fullness of time' (cf. Galatians 4:4)." Meanwhile, John Paul notes, the Church is carrying out the mission of Israel to the nations. He quotes approvingly a Jewish leader who said at a meeting, "I want to thank the Pope for all that the Catholic Church has done over the last two thousand years to make the true God known." We may recall in this connection that the council's great Constitution on the Church, authoritatively setting forth her understanding of herself, is entitled *Lumen Gentium,* referring to the fulfillment of the vocation of Israel to be "a light to the nations."

A useful reference for understanding the state of Catholic teaching is, of course, the *Catechism of the Catholic Church.* The catechism has relatively little to say about Jews and Judaism in the postbiblical period, although, it must be admitted, the subject receives more attention in the catechism than it probably does in the everyday piety, preaching, and catechesis of most Christians. The catechism says, "The people descended from Abraham would be the trustees of the promise made to the patriarchs, the chosen people, called to prepare for that day when God would gather all his children into the unity of the Church." That hint of supersessionism is immediately tempered by reference to the branches being grafted onto the root of Israel. At another point the catechism underscores the Jewish character of the early Church, citing the statement of the apostle James and other elders, "How many thousands there are among the Jews of those who have believed; and they are all zealous for the Law." The catechism's discussion of the Second Coming refers to Romans 11 and "the 'full inclusion' of the Jews in the Messiah's salvation." The fullest statement in the catechism is found under the title "The Church and non-Christians," and deserves quotation: "And when one considers the future, God's People of the Old Covenant and the new People of God tend towards similar goals: expectation of the coming (or the return) of the Messiah who died and rose from the dead and is recognized as Lord and Son of God; the other awaits the coming of a Messiah, whose features remain hidden till the end of time; and the latter waiting is accompanied by the drama of not knowing or of misunderstanding Christ Jesus."

While the catechism is of course an authoritative presentation of Catholic teaching, one misses in its discussion *Nostra Aetate*'s sense of the present-tense relationship of the Church to the Jewish people from which the Church learns and draws sustenance. Nor, in this connection, does the catechism's treatment of eschatological expectation suggest a promised understanding or resolution of differences beyond that which the Church already knows and embodies.

One may usefully contrast Rabbi David Novak's concluding thoughts on "the final redemption" in his book *Jewish-Christian Dialogue:*

> Until that time, we are all travelers passing through a vale of tears until we appear before God in Zion. Jews and Christians begin at the same starting point, and both are convinced that we will meet at the all-mysterious end. Yet we cannot deny that our appointed tasks in this world are very different and must remain so because the covenant is not the same for both of us. It is God alone who will bring us to our unknown destination in a time pleasing to him. . . . Our dialogue might be able to show the world that the hope it needs for its very survival can only be the hope for its final redemption. . . . From creation and revelation comes our faith that God has not and will not abandon us or the world, that the promised redemption is surely yet to come.

Christians believe that the redemption that is surely yet to come has already appeared in the Redeemer, Jesus the Christ. In the End Time, the Messiah will not appear as a stranger. Along the way, we have known his name and named his name. Yet Novak's sense of heightened expectation of something new—as distinct from the confirmation of a completely foregone and foreknown conclusion—seems to me the appropriate mode of eschatological hope also for Christians. Knowing that we do not yet know even as we are known, we know that there is more to be known. Dialogue between Jews and Christians should be marked by an element of curiosity, by shared exploration of what we do not know, and perhaps cannot know until the End Time.

For this reason, too, the words of Jesus—"Salvation is from the Jews"—should have a more prominent place in that continuing exploration. The passage nicely combines the "now" and "not yet" of life lived eschatologically. The "now" is unequivocal. The woman at the well says to him, "I know that Messiah is coming and when he comes he will show us all things." Jesus answers, "I who speak to you am he." The "now" and "not yet" are then joined in the words of Jesus: "The hour is coming when neither on this mountain nor in Jerusalem will you worship the Father. . . . The hour is coming, and now is, when the true worshipers will worship the Father in spirit and truth, for such the Father seeks to worship him."

We find in these words an intimation of the vision at the end of the Book of Revelation: "And I saw no temple in the city, for its temple is the Lord God the Almighty and the Lamb. And the city has no need of sun or moon to shine upon it, for the glory of God is its light, and its lamp is the Lamb. By its light shall the nations walk; and the kings of the earth shall bring their glory into it, and its gates shall never shut by day—and there shall be no night; they shall bring into it the glory and the honor of the nations." That is the mission of Israel fulfilled as *lumen gentium*—light to the world.

Along the way to that fulfillment, Christians and Jews will disagree about whether we can name the name of the Lamb. And when it turns out that we Christians have rightly named the Lamb ahead of time, there will be, as Saint Paul reminds us, no reason for boasting; for in the beginning, all along the way, and in the final consummation, it will be evident to all that the Lamb—which is to say salvation—is from the Jews. Salvation is from the Jews, then, not as a "point of departure," but as the continuing presence and promise of a point of arrival—a point of arrival that we, Christians and Jews, together pray that we will together reach. In that shared prayer is the hope of the world that Babylon is not forever.

In the next chapter we address some of the truths to which Christians and Jews bear witness together. These are truths without which our life in exile is, in the words of Thomas Hobbes, "solitary, poor, nasty, brutish, and short." They are truths with which, in the vision of the prophet Jeremiah, the peace of our place of exile, in which we find our peace, can be approximately secured.

VII

Politics for the Time Being

REMEMBER THE SECOND-CENTURY *Letter to Diognetus* and the observation that Christians who are exiled in a foreign country treat that foreign country as their homeland—for the time being, as everything is for the time being. Without confusing the foreign country with their true home in the New Jerusalem, and while refusing to bow the knee to its foreign gods, they accept the opportunity to play their part as citizens, albeit as dual citizens. This means, among other things, that they take part in the political affairs of their temporary homeland.

Politics is conflictual. That is because the *polis* that is the city of man is not a true community. The crucial distinction here is between society and community. The true community for which human beings were made, the community in which our humanity is finally fulfilled, is a state of living together in the truth. Community depends upon communication, and in a true community, communication is utterly honest, transparent, free of deception and misunderstanding. Obviously, that is not the state of our life together at present. We live in the ruins of Babel. In society we do not live together in the truth because we are not in agreement about the truth. Even those who are convinced that they know the truth—especially those who are convinced that they know the truth—have to say, with Saint Paul, "For now we see in a mirror dimly, but then face to face. Now I know in part; then I shall understand fully, even as I have been fully understood."

Community is *communio* in the truth. In the life of the Church, in communion with Christ, who says of himself, "I am the way, the truth, and the life," we experience a foretaste, a prolepsis, of the community that is to be. So it is that in the Eucharist, which is the prolepsis of the Wedding Feast of the Lamb, we experience the genuinely "new politics" of the new *polis* that is the City of God. But it is only a foretaste that whets our appetite for, and sacramentally sustains us on the way toward, that final destination. Having tasted of what is to be, we say with Thomas Becket in T. S. Eliot's *Murder in the Cathedral,*

> *I have had a tremor of bliss, a wink of heaven, a whisper,*
> *And I would no longer be denied; all things*
> *Proceed to a joyful consummation.*

Short of that consummation, we live not in true community but in society. Society is not universal but is composed of societies, of *us* and *them,* of rival identities and aspirations, of ambitions and interests in a state of constant negotiation, whether peacefully or through violence. Thomas Becket died as a martyr to the truth, and the politics of society is marked by rival claims to truth in conflict. We seek cooperation, but the cooperation we seek is typically in the service of our goals, which are in competition with the goals of others. A staple in public life is the political actor who claims to be nonpartisan or postpartisan. Claims of this nature meet with a robust skepticism on the part of thoughtful citizens, and well they should. Such skepticism can, but need not, lead to a cynical view of the politics of the earthly city. A disciplined skepticism about the politics of this or any society is not cynicism, but wisdom.

It is a wisdom that is regularly celebrated as the genius of the American constitutional order. This is an order that allows for political interventions animated by lofty aspirations. One might even say that it is inspired by such aspirations. At the same time, however, it is constructed on the assumption that aspirations are tethered to interests. This is commonly called "realism." Realism does not deny that there is such a thing as "The Public Interest," but it recognizes that it is usually best secured by the contest of particular interests typically claiming to be in the service of The Public Interest. Partisans of particular interests sometimes describe opposing interests as factions.

In *The Federalist*, Madison describes a faction as "a number of citizens, whether amounting to a minority or majority of the whole, who are united and actuated by some common impulse of passion, or of interest, adverse to the rights of other citizens, or to the permanent and aggregate interests of the community." In Madison's vocabulary, "faction" is a bad thing. In today's political reality, we tend to view those opposing us as "factions," while we prefer to believe that our purposes are advanced by "coalitions" in service to the interests of the community, which we call the common good.

The passions of politics—what Augustine called *libido dominandi*—are inevitable. The American founders had no utopian delusions about establishing a community of interests and desires harmoniously coordinated in service to the common good. This constitutional order is not a machine that runs by itself. Rather, as Madison and others understood, this is an order of government in which faction is checked by faction in the hope, first of all, that their proponents will not destroy one another, and second, that their open-ended rivalry might conduce to something that approximates the common good. The national motto, *E pluribus unum*, refers not only to many peoples becoming one but also to many purposes vigorously pursued ending up, through ways usually circuitous and unforeseen, in serving all. That at least is the idea.

This is not to deny that there may be visionary and great-souled leaders who, rising above particular interests, seek only to advance the common good. But it is to say, first, that such leaders are exceedingly rare; second, that this constitutional order does not depend on their being in frequent supply; and third, that anyone who claims to be such a leader will meet with a strong measure of incredulity. Politics is not so much a matter of rising above interests but of making the arguments and showing the ways in which interests can compete, overlap, and sometimes converge in serving the common good.

The goal of the American political order, wrote Father John Courtney Murray, is to maintain a circumstance in which citizens are "locked in civil argument." My argument in the 1984 book *The Naked Public Square* has frequently been misunderstood on this score, especially by those whose political activity is religiously motivated. The alternative to the naked public square—meaning public life stripped of religion and religiously grounded argument—is not the *sacred* public square, but the *civil* public square. The sacred public square is located in the New Jerusalem. The best that can be done in Babylon is to maintain, usually with great difficulty, a civil public square.

In the civil public square, all have a right to participate—not only because they are citizens so entitled by this constitutional order, but also, and more fundamentally, because we recognize that they are possessed of a human dignity that cannot be denied without threatening the ever fragile earthly city on which we all depend. In the high-spirited political contests that mark a vibrantly democratic society, the imagery of warfare is sometimes invoked. Thus politicians are sometimes described as "happy warriors" smiting the enemy hip and thigh. Such imagery is best kept in close check, however. In recent years there has been much discussion of the "culture wars." Politics seems to be warfare carried on by other means, and sometimes threatening to edge over into warfare itself. There is no denying the intense conflict over differing visions of American culture—over the ideas and ideals that ought to shape our common life. For the sake of maintaining the civil public square, culture warriors on all sides of ideas and ideals in conflict are called to sharpen their arguments rather than their swords.

This is especially the case with respect to the inescapable interaction of religion and politics. There is considerable truth in the observation that politics is primarily a function of culture, that at the heart of culture is morality, and that at the heart of morality are those commanding truths typically associated with religion. I expect it is true in every society, but it is certainly true in this society, that politics and religion can be distinguished but never separated. Unless tempered by the virtue of civility, the metaphor of "culture wars," in which commanding truths are pitted against each other, can easily lead to a circumstance in which politics degenerates into warfare that is not merely metaphorical. The untempered clash of commanding truths in conflict can degenerate into religious warfare, which in America means not warfare between religions but between opposing visions of the common good prosecuted with religious fervor, with one side unfurling its battle banners against "theocracy" and the other against "the dictatorship of secularism."

One encounters the frequent assertion that politics inspired by religious belief is prone to fanaticism, and there is ample historical support for that claim. Today this danger is driven home by the jihadist terrorism of radical Islam. Fanaticism takes many forms, however. The word "fanatic," we do well to remember, comes from the Latin *fanum,* meaning a temple of the gods. The politics of those who live in the temples of Babylon takes on an ultimate significance. There is no appeal, no hope, beyond service to the ideas and ideals that are the deities of the present order. (Although, as we shall see in the final chapter, for the morally reflective such devotion to the deities of the present is not so complete as it sometimes seems.) It is very different with those who know themselves to be in exile from a better city. For them, the possibilities and urgencies of the politics of Babylon are not ultimate but, at most, penultimate. A hope that is rightly described as eschatological both inspires and tempers their political engagement. Knowing that they will be held responsible for what can be done, they are freed from attempting what cannot be done in a city that is only for the time being.

Politics engages many questions, but there are no questions that so deeply agitate the politics of our time as those touching upon what it means to be a human being. One might protest that this is not properly a political question at all, and there is considerable merit to that objection. When, however, the question is put in terms of who is a bearer of rights that we, as a society, are obliged to respect, it is turned into a political question and must be addressed as such. And so we have center-staged in today's political arena what are commonly called the "life questions." They are typically posed in terms of a conflict between individual freedom, on the one side, and the dignity of the human person, on the other. But the arguments invoking freedom and those invoking dignity can cut in surprising directions.

The "life questions"—and, more generally, the questions engaged by bioethics about present and proposed technological manipulations of the *humanum*, of what it means to be human—are certainly not the only questions agitating our politics. I believe a persuasive argument can be made, however, that they are the most important questions—that, if we do not get these right, we are unlikely to get right many other questions of great moment. Moreover, these are the questions that most explicitly display the nature of politics, along with the possibilities and limitations of politics in the earthly city.

There is in these discussions a great dispute over the idea of *human dignity*. How useful is the concept of human dignity in considering a wide range of issues in bioethics? There are those who take the position that *human dignity* is little more than a shibboleth that clouds clear thinking about our powers and responsibilities to shape the human future. Asking whether an idea such as human dignity is useful immediately invites the question, Useful for what? In this context, we are asking whether it is morally useful. And to ask whether it is morally useful is, as we shall see, to ask whether it is politically useful. This is the great question over which we are "locked in civil argument."

In the history of our civilization's reflections on ethics and morality, it is commonly said that the most elementary maxim is "Do good and avoid evil." For purposes pertinent to bioethics and much else, this can also be phrased as "Do right and avoid wrong." The first principle of practical moral reason, in obedience to that maxim, is to direct one's will in accord with the human good. It would seem obvious that the human good is served by respect for human dignity. But this obviously is not obvious to all. The argument is sharpened if we speak not of human dignity but of *the dignity of the human person*. The phrase *human dignity* may suggest the human collective and include efforts such as taking technological charge of the evolution of the human species. *The dignity of the human person* places the accent on the individual—although, to be sure, the individual situated in society, and, one hopes, in society that aspires to being community.

The dignity of the human person entails an important, although limited, measure of autonomy. Dignity as autonomy features strongly in, for instance, arguments for "death with dignity." In the realm of morality, however, where we consider our duties toward others, the dignity of the human person is affirmed not in the assertion of our autonomy but in attending to our duties to protect those who lack autonomy, or whose autonomy is gravely limited. Thus it is said that, in medicine as in other activities, the first rule is "Do no harm." That first rule enjoins us to protect and nurture something that is not necessarily or demonstrably good *for* this or *for* that but is good simply in its being. The rule "Do no harm" is perceived by some to be a limit on scientific and technological progress, and, of course, it is intended to be exactly that.

Not for nothing are the biblical commandments on how we are to treat others framed in the negative. Cutting through our rationalizations and indulgence of appealing possibilities, they declare, Do *not* do this and do *not* do that. Proposed positives that do not rest upon secure negatives are not to be trusted. "Do no harm" is a frankly and unapologetically moral placing of limits on those who are driven by what is aptly described as the scientific or technological imperative in the service of their understanding of progress. In Chapter 3, we examined the limits and possibilities of moral progress. There have been great advances, and there will likely be many more, in what Francis Bacon called "the relief of man's estate." It is precisely the business of ethical and moral reason to make normative judgments regarding present and proposed measures aimed at such relief. This is true with respect to the dignity of the human person and with respect to more ambitious proposals aimed not so much at relieving as at transforming "man's estate." (When reflecting on these questions, it is good to have at hand C. S. Lewis's *The Abolition of Man.*)

The ill-defined discipline of bioethics has not served us well in understanding these questions. Militating against the task of normative moral judgment is not only the scientific and technological imperative, with all the fame and glory that come with "breakthrough" achievements, but also the weight of inestimable financial interests. Think, for instance, of what those who can pay will pay for a significant extension of their life span or for the "perfect baby." It is only somewhat jaded to observe that institutions with the greatest vested interest in morally dubious advances have recruited the best bioethicists that money can buy. This is said not to impugn motives but to clarify the morally suspect convergence of interests.

Bioethics as an intellectual institution is, in significant part, an industry for the production of rationalized—sometimes elegantly rationalized—permission slips in the service of the technological imperative joined to the pursuit of fame and wealth. Such permission slips are also issued in the service of what some believe to be the relief of suffering and the enhancement of man's estate. Even when bioethics is conducted with intellectual and moral integrity, however, a question must be raised about the nature of the authority of those who are called bioethicists. This touches on politics and political legitimacy in addressing bioethical controversies.

International agreements and declarations in the aftermath of World War II often spoke of the dignity of the human person, and it is frequently noted that these usages do not offer clear and unambiguous guidance in bioethical controversies. In a book published by the President's Council on Bioethics, it is observed, correctly, that in such international statements "the meaning, content, and foundations of human dignity are never explicitly defined. Instead, the affirmation of human dignity in these documents reflects a political consensus among groups that may well have quite different beliefs about what human dignity means, where it comes from, and what it entails. In effect, 'human dignity' serves here as a placeholder for 'whatever it is about human beings that entitles them to basic human rights and freedoms.'" The council adds, however, that "this practice makes a good deal of sense."

And it does make a great deal of sense. In a world indelibly marked and marred by the Holocaust, the Gulag Archipelago, Mao's Great Leap Forward, and myriad other crimes against humanity, a political consensus as a placeholder against great evils, no matter how intellectually rickety its structure, is not to be scorned. Harvard law professor Mary Ann Glendon has described the ways in which the drafters of the United Nations' Universal Declaration of Human Rights were keenly aware that their goal was a political consensus, not a philosophical or moral treatise on human nature and the rights and dignities attending human nature. Given the enormous cultural, religious, intellectual, and ideological diversity of those involved, a political consensus was a great achievement. While rights and freedoms are positively asserted, they are largely defined negatively against the background of evils to which the declaration says, in effect, "Never again!" Thus was the morally elementary rule "Do no harm" given new urgency and specificity.

Nor should it be thought that a political consensus is somehow inferior to a coherent treatise on the moral and philosophical foundations of human dignity. In a world that continues to be characterized by *libido dominandi*—the unbridled lust for power and glory—politics is an instrument for the restraint of great evil. In ethics, and in bioethics specifically, politics is frequently seen as an alien intrusion on, or a poor substitute for, the search for clear and unambiguous ethical theory. But the search for guidance through the controversies besetting us is precisely a political task. Politics is not a distraction from moral reflection, nor is it an intrusion on moral reflection. Politics is—among many other things that politics is—an exercise in moral reflection.

Aristotle's *Nicomachean Ethics* and his *Politics* are both discourses on morality. From them we can derive this summary definition of politics: *Politics is free persons deliberating the question, How ought we to order our life together?* The *ought* in that suggested definition clearly indicates that politics is (in its nature, if not always in its practice) a moral enterprise. As noted earlier, our political vocabulary—what is fair or unfair, what is just or unjust, what serves the common good—is inescapably a moral vocabulary. Contra David Hume and many others, it is not so obvious that an *ought* cannot be derived from an *is.* In the ordinary experience of individuals and communities, it is done with great regularity. Neither agreement nor consensus is required on all the details of "whatever it is about human beings that entitles them to basic human rights and freedoms." People who explain the "whatever it is" in quite different ways can agree on what ought and ought not be done to human beings.

The political consensus of the Universal Declaration of 1948, although important, undoubtedly rests on a philosophically "thin" account of the dignity of the human person. That is in large part because the "international community" is not a community. It is a conglomerate of societies, and pieces of societies, ostensibly represented by states and state-like institutions. For more than a few of the nearly 200 member states of the United Nations, for instance, their chief claim to being nations is their membership in the United Nations. The "international community" as institutionalized in the United Nations and other organizations is not, in Aristotle's sense of the term, a *polis* in which free persons deliberate the question of how we ought to order our lives together.

To be sure, there are many and interesting debates about whether the United States or its several states qualify as a *polis.* We need not go into the details of those debates; it is beyond dispute that our constitutional order presents itself as a political community deliberating its right ordering on the basis of the political sovereignty of "the people" exercised through the specified means of representative democracy. The foundational principle here is the statement of the Declaration of Independence that just government is derived from the consent of the governed. In a representative democracy such as ours, how that consent is given and how the people exercise their sovereignty is typically a rough and raucous process of contending interests, ambitions, and aspirations driven by the power of money and media.

There is no point in attempting to idealize the process by which we deliberate how we ought to order our life together. Seldom does it seem very deliberative. Whether in elections or in the work of legislatures, it bears little resemblance to an academic seminar in moral theory. And yet, for all the manipulative marketing of slogans and images, and for all the manifestly self-seeking interests in play, we do make decisions about the common good using this particular deliberative process, within the bounds of this constitutional order. Or, if "the common good" sounds too lofty, we can put it another way: In the absence of a more comprehensive agreement about the common good, we provisionally establish a measure of political equilibrium by following this process.

The question of the dignity of the human person is rightly understood as a political question. It is inescapably a political question. The resolution (always provisional and open to revision) of the great majority of political disputes does not ordinarily require delving into the foundational truths explored by philosophy, ethics, and theology. Our political discourse is guided, and frequently misguided, by custom, habits, and tacit understandings. Proponents of natural law theory rely heavily on moral reasoning attuned to "those things that we cannot *not* know." And of course other theories are advanced, both because they are held to be true and because they are thought to be useful for purposes of political persuasion. Sometimes for one reason, sometimes for the other, and sometimes for both.

In general, our political life is not heavily burdened by theory, or at least not by the explication of theory. That is because knowing and judging the good things of human life is not so burdened. Most people most of the time think they know what makes for human flourishing, beginning with their own lives and the lives of their families and then extended by common feeling to the lives of others. This is often called common sense. The prejudice favoring common sense is generally sound. At least it is a prejudice presupposed in democratic theory and practice.

To say that the practice of democratic politics is not heavily burdened with theory does not mean that arguments are unimportant. While the manipulation of images and media spin often seem to be in control, people want to believe that they make decisions based on arguments that "speak to the issues." It may well be that many, perhaps most, people make their decisions on the basis of image manipulation and media spin and then adopt the arguments that support their decisions. But it is part of democratic duty to resist the temptation to cynicism on this score. Respect for the dignity of others includes treating them as rational creatures capable of being persuaded by rational argument, even in the face of frequent evidence to the contrary.

This is notably the case with respect to policy questions touching on the dignity of the human person, and the most obvious example is abortion and the issues inseparably tied to abortion. I believe it is fair to say that the most consequential political event of the past half-century in the United States was the Supreme Court's *Roe v. Wade* and *Doe v. Bolton* decisions of January 1973. Numerous political analysts have described how those decisions have dramatically reconfigured the nation's cultural and political life. And, of course, those decisions are intimately tied to many other hot-button issues in bioethics. As an act of "raw judicial power" (the words are those of Justice Byron White in his dissenting opinion), *Roe* and *Doe* removed a preeminently political, which is to say moral, question from public deliberation. The abortion decisions were a profoundly antipolitical act and are accurately described as instances of the judicial usurpation of politics. By attempting to remove the question of the protection of unborn children from public debate, the Court turned it into something very much like the vortex of American politics.

Beginning in the 1960s, there was much agitation for what was called the "liberalization of abortion law." The issue was vigorously disputed, and those on all sides of the question expressed their surprise, both delighted and outraged, when on January 22, 1973, the Supreme Court, in *Roe* and *Doe,* wiped off the books of all fifty states any and every protection of unborn human lives. Those who were delighted by the decisions, which at the time included all the elite institutions of the political class, declared that the Supreme Court had "settled" the abortion question. But, of course, it quickly became the most unsettled question in our public life.

The Court revisited the question in its 1992 *Planned Parenthood v. Casey* decision and once again astonished many on all sides by declaring, in effect, that it was un-American to disagree with the Supreme Court. The words of the Court majority provide a succinct definition of what is meant by the judicial usurpation of politics: "Where, in the performance of its judicial duties, the Court decides a case in such a way as to resolve the sort of intensely divisive controversy reflected in Roe . . . its decision has a dimension that the resolution of the normal case does not carry. It is the dimension present whenever the Court's interpretation of the Constitution calls the contending sides of a national controversy to end their national division by accepting a common mandate rooted in the Constitution."

Needless to say, the millions of Americans who disagree with *Roe*—according to some survey research, a growing majority of Americans—did not accept the Court's dictate to cease and desist in their disagreement. The Court majority in *Roe* and subsequent abortion decisions never went so far as to claim that the Constitution speaks explicitly to the question of abortion. And, contra the Court, the moral and legal question is not about when a human life begins. That is a biological and medical question on which there is no serious dispute. The crucial question is: At what point in its existence ought we, and for what reasons ought we, to recognize that a human life should be protected in law?

On this issue, if no other, Peter Singer has it right. As the noted Princeton ethicist and advocate of infanticide said in a June 20, 2005, letter to the *New York Times* rebuking former New York Governor Mario Cuomo for his confused thinking about abortion: "The crucial moral question is not when human life begins, but when human life reaches the point at which it merits protection. . . . Unless we separate these two questions—when does life begin, and when does it merit protection?—we are unlikely to achieve any clarity about the moral status of embryos."

That moral question is also and unavoidably a political question. One might make the case that it is the most fundamental of political questions. If politics is deliberating how we ought to order our life together, there can hardly be a more basic question than this: Who belongs to the *we*? Although ostensibly removing it from politics, the Court's abortion decisions forced into the political arena an issue that was thought to have been settled in the centuries of civilizational tradition of which our polity is part: namely, that it is morally wrong and rightly made unlawful to deliberately kill innocent human beings. If a principle is established by which some indisputably human lives do not warrant the protections traditionally associated with the dignity of the human person—because of their size, location, dependency, level of development, or burdensomeness to others—it would seem that there are numerous candidates for the application of the principle, beginning with the radically handicapped, both physically and mentally, not to mention millions of the aged and severely debilitated in our nation's nursing homes.

It may be objected that *of course* we as a people are not about to embark on such a program of extermination. To think we might do so is simply bizarre. And as a culturally and politically contingent fact of our present social circumstance, that is true. But under the regime of *Roe,* we have no "clear and unambiguous" agreed-on rule precluding such horrors. We do have in our constituting texts, notably in the Declaration of Independence, a commitment to natural rights, and we do have deeply entrenched in our culture and politics a concept of the dignity of the human person.

The question, then, is this: Who belongs to the community for which we as a community accept responsibility, including the responsibility to protect, along with other natural rights, their right to life? This is a preeminently political question. It is not a question to be decided by bioethicists. Bioethicists, by virtue of their disciplined attention to such questions, are in a position to help inform political deliberations and decisions about these matters, but these questions are—rightly and of necessity—to be decided politically. They are rightly so decided because our constitutional order vests political sovereignty in the people, who exercise that sovereignty through prescribed means of representation. They are of necessity so decided because in this society the views of moral philosophers—whether trained as such in the academy or acting as such on the bench—are not deemed to be determinative. Witness the democratic nonratification of the Supreme Court's imposition of the unlimited abortion license.

To say that such decisions are rightly decided politically is not to say that the resulting decisions will always be morally right. Those who disagree with the decisions that are made must make their case in the political arena. The product of bioethics may be prescriptive in theory—resulting in "clear and unambiguous" guidelines—but, in this constitutional order, it has to be persuasive in practice. In fact, of course, disagreements among moral philosophers, including bioethicists, are as strong as those found in the general public, if not stronger.

In the happy absence of philosopher-kings, everybody enters the process of debate, deliberation, and decision equipped only with the powers of reason and persuasion. Obviously, not everybody enters on equal terms, since powers of persuasion, access to the means of persuasion, and the audiences inclined to be persuaded are far from equal. This is a highly unsatisfactory circumstance in which the achievement of clear and unambiguous rules is rare, and a political consensus resting on a moral point of reference as a "placeholder" may be, as noted earlier, deemed a great achievement.

One such point of reference is the dignity of the human person—construed not, or not primarily, as the assertion of the rights of the autonomous, but as the obligation to protect those whose autonomy is limited. It is complained that those who defend that point of reference have an unfair advantage, in that it is so widely shared in our culture. They are engaged, it is said, not in moral or ethical argument, but in politics. As suggested earlier, however, politics *is* moral argument about how we ought to order our life together. After the June 1953 uprising in East Germany, the secretary of the Writers Union distributed leaflets declaring that the people had lost the confidence of the government and it would take redoubled efforts to win it back. To which the playwright Bertolt Brecht is supposed to have responded, "Would it not be easier in that case for the government to dissolve the people and elect another?" Not infrequently, bioethicists, moral philosophers, and judges appear to want to follow Brecht's advice and dissolve the people who have proved so recalcitrant in resisting their wisdom.

The people who are the American *polis* are deeply attached to the concept of the dignity of the human person. For those who are morally devoted to this constitutional order and the means it provides for addressing the *res publica,* that is a factor of considerable significance. Yet there are those who contend that such popular attachments are prejudices or unreflective biases that have no legitimate place in authentically *public* discourse. Well known is the exclusion, commonly associated with John Rawls, of "comprehensive accounts" from authentically public discourse. That exclusion is most rigorously asserted when such comprehensive accounts are perceived to be "religious" in nature.

The moral authority of those who would make the rules for what is to be admitted and what is to be excluded from public discourse is far from clear to many students of these arguments and is totally baffling to the people who are the public. The perfectly understandable suspicion is that there is a self-serving dynamic in the efforts of some to appoint themselves the gatekeepers and border patrol of the public square, admitting some arguments and excluding others. The exclusion of comprehensive accounts—especially when they are religious or associated with a religious tradition—gives a monopoly on the public square to accounts that are nonreligious or antireligious in character. Such accounts are, in fact, no less comprehensive. Conflicts that are described as being between reason and tradition are typically conflicts between different traditions of reason, each invoking its own authorities.

In the comprehensive accounts that would proscribe other comprehensive accounts, especially if they are perceived as religious in nature, the operative assumption is typically atheism. This is certainly not to say that all who support such proscriptions are atheists. It is to say that, in their moral reasoning, they are *methodological* atheists. Only those arguments are to be admitted to public deliberation that proceed *as if* God did not exist. This is a nonrational prejudice to which the great majority of Americans do not adhere. They believe it is a great deal more rational to proceed as if God does exist. In any event, they do so proceed. The politically sovereign people are free to acknowledge, and generally do acknowledge, a sovereignty higher than their own and to give public expression to that acknowledgment.

For most purposes in the ordering of our common life, it is neither necessary nor wise to invoke an account of moral reality beyond what is required for the resolution of the issue at hand. Explicitly moral arguments are not to be expanded or multiplied beyond necessity. And the temptation to define as a "moral issue" any issue about which we feel strongly is to be firmly resisted. On most issues, a sustainable measure of political equilibrium can be achieved by appeal to a widely shared and "thin" account of moral reality that is far less than comprehensive. This is frequently not the case, however, in questions related to bioethics.

People who are themselves devoutly religious may in the public square advance arguments that are not distinctively religious in character. This is notably the case with proponents of natural law theory. They proceed on the basis that human beings are naturally endowed with a rational capacity to discern the truth, including the moral truth, of things. In public argument, they avoid making religious or theological claims, contending that agreement on the ultimate sources and ends of human reason is not necessary to the exercise of human reason.

Contrary to whatever the critics of natural law theory may say, the theory and its practice are not discredited by the observation that many, if not most, of the practitioners do in fact have definite ideas on sources and ends. Nor is the theory discredited by being widely perceived as a distinctively Catholic theory, which it is not. To the extent it is perceived that way, however, its proponents can readily respond that a distinctively Catholic contribution to our common life is to have preserved a universal understanding of reason that, being universal, is in no way peculiarly Catholic. It is an understanding that has strong roots in the Aristotelian view of politics and public discourse under discussion here.

Not all Americans are as abstemious as natural law theorists are when it comes to unfurling in public their ultimate and comprehensive truth claims. For the great majority of Americans, religion and morality are inextricably intertwined. Moreover, public arguments involve different publics or different parts of the public. To those publics who are presumed to share their comprehensive account of reality in its fullness, proponents of this position or that will make the arguments that they think will be most persuasive. Whether in public argument one invokes Scripture or an explicitly Christian or Jewish moral tradition is a prudential judgment. The question is whether such invocations will help persuade or alienate the people one wants to convince.

It is sometimes said that in the public square religious folk have an obligation to present their arguments in a form that is genuinely *public,* meaning that they will be accessible to all reasonable parties. This is a demand that is both unreasonable and unfair. It is a demand that is not imposed on any other sector or institution of society. Labor unions, business, environmental groups, and a host of others are expected to advance their interests and to advance arguments in support of their interests. The Southern Baptist Convention and the United Methodist Church are equally free to frame their arguments as they see fit. Although they have that right, however, it is a matter of prudence to put forth arguments that will be effective, meaning arguments that will persuade those whom they want to persuade. Some advocates will clinch their arguments with "The Bible says so." They will do so because that is a clinching argument for significant parts of the American public. Such invocations of authority, whether religious or not, are inevitable. Those who have a problem with it have a problem with democracy. (Obviously, many thoughtful people, from ancient times to the present, have had grave reservations about democracy.)

There is, of course, a necessary concern about unbridled populism, raw majoritarianism, and the dangers of demagoguery. The framers of our constitutional order were keenly aware of these dangers. Hence our system of representation, checks and balances, staggered elections, vetoes, overrides, judicial review, and other mechanisms conducive to a more sober deliberation of how we ought to order our life together. While this intentionally complex order slows the course of turning agitations into law and public policy, it in no way restricts the arguments that can be made. Nor, needless to say, does it guarantee that the best arguments will prevail.

Demagogic agitation for specific laws or policies is sometimes employed, for instance, by identifying one's policy preferences with the will of God. Such appeals are usually limited to audiences where it is thought they might be persuasive. There is also the demagoguery of appeals to the more general public that—for instance, in the controversy over using and destroying embryonic human life in scientific research—cruelly exploit human suffering and exaggerated or unfounded hopes for cures.

Such demagoguery was widespread in arguments about stem-cell research prior to November 2007, when it was announced that scientists had discovered a way to obtain the desired stem cells without creating and destroying embryos. This is a dramatic instance of scientific advance checking the technological imperative that was driving support for embryo-destructive research, fetal farming, and related measures claimed to be essential for new therapies. As encouraging as this particular instance is, we cannot always count on scientific hubris being checked by scientific achievement. As discussed in Chapter 3, the ideology of "progress" is exceedingly powerful in its seductiveness and will always have to be engaged by the clarity and force of argument in defense of human dignity.

Demagoguery in support of unethical scientific practices will always be with us. Again, our constitutional order is not a machine that runs of itself. It depends on the cultivation of restraint, civility, and disciplined reason, which are always in short supply. And we do well to keep in mind that the wisest of our public philosophers, from Alexis de Tocqueville onward, cautioned not only against the tyranny of the majority but also against the tyranny of the minority. Today that caution is pertinent to the minority that would impose a rule that authentically public discourse be methodologically atheistic. Restraint, civility, and disciplined reason are seriously undermined by the hostility to "comprehensive accounts" in our public discourse—especially if they are perceived to be religious in nature.

In most intellectual enterprises, and not least in ethics, there is a propensity to emulate the methodologies and exactitude associated with the physical sciences. Philosopher Thomas Nagel writes:

> This reductionist dream is nourished by the extraordinary success of the physical sciences in our time, not least in their recent application to the understanding of life through molecular biology. It is natural to try to take any successful intellectual method as far as it will go. Yet the impulse to find an explanation of everything in physics has over the last fifty years gotten out of control. The concepts of physical science provide a very special, and partial, description of the world that experience reveals to us. It is the world with all subjective consciousness, sensory appearances, thought, value, purpose, and will left out. What remains is the mathematically describable order of things and events in space and time. . . . We have more than one form of understanding. Different forms of understanding are needed for different kinds of subject matter. The great achievements of physical science do not make it capable of encompassing everything, from mathematics to ethics to the experiences of a living animal.

The concept of the dignity of the human person was arrived at, and is today sustained, by such a different form of understanding. It is a form of understanding that is carefully reasoned, and frankly moral, and, for most people who affirm it, it is in fact, if not by theoretical necessity, inseparable from a comprehensive account that is unapologetically acknowledged as religious. The hostility to admitting this account to public discourse is long-standing.

Indeed, it has long been argued by some that moral references should be eliminated altogether from law and public policy, that ours is a strictly procedural polity devoted only to means and prescinding from ends, and especially from overtly moral ends. Oliver Wendell Holmes Jr. famously wrote that it would be a great benefit "if every word of moral significance could be banished from the law altogether, and other words adopted which should convey legal ideas uncolored by anything outside the law."

But, of course, it was by ideas and experiences outside the law that the concept of the dignity of the human person was enshrined in the law. The word "enshrined" is used advisedly, indicating the sacred sources of that dignity. In religious thought, and in Christian thought specifically, the dignity of the human person has become the touchstone of ethical reflection. Pope John Paul the Great wrote on several occasions that the entirety of Catholic social doctrine rests on the understanding of the dignity of the human person. The *Catechism of the Catholic Church* devotes no fewer than twenty-three pages to explaining the concept and its implications. It is an explanation that in its essentials is embraced also by non-Catholic Christians, as is evident, for instance, in the 2006 statement of Evangelicals and Catholics Together, "That They May Have Life." It is a concept firmly grounded in the Jewish tradition and—although not without troubling ambiguities—in Islam.

That concept, on which almost all Americans rely, with varying degrees of reflectiveness and consistency, in deliberating how we ought to order our life together, can be briefly summarized in this way: *A human being is a person possessed of a dignity we are obliged to respect at every point of development, debilitation, or decline by virtue of being created in the image and likeness of God. Endowed with the spiritual principle of the soul, with reason and with free will, the destiny of the person who acts in accord with moral conscience in obedience to the truth is nothing less than eternal union with God. This is the dignity of the human person that is to be respected, defended, and indeed revered.*

That is beyond doubt a very comprehensive, or "thick," account of the dignity of the human person. I have referred to the political sovereignty of "the people" in our constitutional order. The location of sovereignty—the authority to which the *polis* holds itself finally accountable—has in the post–World War II era been, one might say, personalized. Ours is a period that Karl Barth, the most influential Protestant theologian of the past century, described as one of "disillusioned sovereignty." The great disillusionment is with the sovereignty of the state. The practitioners of the unbridled technological imperative in our day are eager to obtain the license and, if possible, the support of the state for their purposes. In this way, they live in an older world in which there is no appeal beyond or against the state.

If one had asked almost all Enlightenment thinkers of the eighteenth century what is sovereign, they would not have answered "reason" or "the individual" or "science." The unhesitating answer would have been "the state." The darkest and most relentless depiction of the modern political project was offered by Thomas Hobbes. He taught that the incarnate and resurrected God-man who lives and governs is to be replaced in the temporal world by a mortal god (*deus mortalis*)—a machinelike man, mythologically known as the Leviathan. Engraved on the title page of the 1651 edition of his book by that title is Job 41:24: *Non est potestas super terram quae comparetur ei*—"There is upon the earth no power like his."

After Auschwitz and the Gulag Archipelago, we cannot read those words without a moral shudder. We must insist that here is on earth Leviathan's like and, indeed, his sovereign: the human person. The concept of the dignity of the human person may be a "placeholder" in international covenants, but in the American political experiment, when public discourse is not arbitrarily constricted by methodological atheism, it is, with respect to bioethics and other matters, a concept of great moral moment, a concept richly and rationally elaborated in our civic and religious traditions and claiming overwhelming public support. It is, in sum, a concept that is indispensable to the political task of deliberating and deciding how we ought to order our life together.

Such deliberation and decision will in our time of exile always be inadequate, provisional, and for the time being. That is because, as noted at the beginning of this chapter, we live in a society that is, as is true of any temporal society, far short of the community that we seek. Genuine community, which is nothing less than *communio* in the fullness of truth, awaits the fulfillment of a promise that is beyond the possibilities of history. All moral reason and all moral action reaches toward, and is contingent upon, that fulfillment. This is true not only for Christians and Jews, who understand themselves to be in Babylonian exile. It is true for all who bear the dignity and the burden of being human that moral reason and moral action is—in the final analysis and therefore all along the way—*eschatological.* Which is to say we cannot live except we live in hope. In the next and final chapter I hope to show why that is the case for all of us.

VIII

Hope and Hopelessness

LIFE FEEDS ON hope, and hope is by definition hope for something better, however variously *better* may be conceived. It may also be the hope to return to something better. To believe that there once was something better will seem like a conservative sentiment, until we remember that the radical traditions running from Rousseau through Marx promised the restoration of something like a "state of nature" in which we could be freed from the artificial distortions of social custom and economic exploitation.

Those whose lives have been graced by the reading and rereading of Kenneth Grahame's *The Wind in the Willows* will not forget the moment when Mr. Mole, running from danger with Mr. Rat, remembers home, "when suddenly the summons reached him, and took him like an electric shock."

> It was one of those mysterious fairy calls from out of the void that suddenly reached Mole in the darkness,

> making him tingle through and through with its familiar appeal, even while as yet he could not clearly remember what it was. He stopped dead in his tracks, his nose searching hither and thither in its efforts to recapture the fine filament, the telegraphic current, that had so strongly moved him. A moment, and he had caught it again; and with it this time came recollection in fullest flood. Home! That was what they meant, those caressing appeals, those soft touches wafted through the air, those invisible little hands pulling and tugging, all one way! . . . The home had been happy with him, too, evidently, and was missing him, and wanted him back, and was telling him so, through his nose, sorrowfully, reproachfully, but with no bitterness or anger; only with plaintive reminder that it was there, and wanted him.

In some world religions as well as in the improvised spiritualities of a postmodern time, the Great Return is a prominent theme. Somewhere, back there, is a world lost and a world to be rediscovered and perhaps retrieved. Such is the charm of fairy tales. Did not we all, a long time ago, live in the Shire of J. R. R. Tolkien's gentle hobbits? The psychotherapies of the past hundred years have not been remiss in exploring the revelations and healing power to be discovered in returning to childhood, and even to the womb. As with Mr. Mole, as with all the myths of the Great Return, the longing is for home. As also with the children of Israel in exile:

> *By the waters of Babylon*
> *there we sat down and wept,*
> *when we remembered Zion . . .*

If I forget you, O Jerusalem,
let my right hand wither!
Let my tongue cleave to the roof of my mouth
if I do not remember you,
if I do not set Jerusalem
above my highest joy!

We remember Jerusalem. So one might say that life feeds not on hope but on memory. Yet the return to the remembered, the restoration of the remembered, is hope. The return or restoration is in the hoped-for future. What has been will be again, or, even better, will be for the first time in a fullness of possibilities never to be lost again. Life feeds on hope.

In the Christian tradition it is said that hope is a "theological virtue." That is true also of faith and love. "Faith, hope, and love," writes Saint Paul, "these three abide. And the greatest of these is love." Virtue is from the Latin *virtus,* meaning "strength." Christians took over from Plato and Aristotle the idea of the four cardinal, or chief, virtues: prudence, temperance, courage (that is, fortitude), and justice. These are said to be the "human virtues" (or "natural virtues") of which we are all capable simply because we are human. It is different with faith, hope, and love. They must be received as gifts, and another word for "gift" is "grace." Grace is a gift of God. Grace is understood theologically, from which it follows that faith, hope, and love are theological virtues.

In his splendid little book *On Hope,* Josef Pieper, an astute disciple of Thomas Aquinas, writes: "It would never occur to a philosopher, unless he were also a

Christian, to describe hope as a virtue. For hope is either a theological virtue or not a virtue at all. It becomes a virtue by becoming a theological virtue." To be sure, the state of hopefulness is better than that of despair, but hopefulness is often no more than a psychological disposition commonly called "optimism." Optimism is not a virtue. Optimism is simply a matter of optics, of seeing what we want to see and not seeing what we don't want to see. Hope is only hope when it is hope with eyes wide open to all that challenges hope. Thus hope is sometimes "hope against hope." Paul writes of our father Abraham, "Hoping against hope, he believed, and thus became the father of many nations." Pieper chooses as the epigraph of his reflection on hope the words of Job in his innocent suffering, "Although he slay me, yet will I trust him."

Our circumstance in this life is *status viatoris*—that is, we are in a state of being on the way, pilgrims. We are also *homo viator,* people on the way, and to be on the way is to live in hope of arriving. It is not only Christians, however, who are in *status viatoris.* To be on the way is intrinsic to the human condition. All human beings, as we shall see, live by hope, and thus the line between natural and theological virtue is not quite so clear as it might at first seem. The *Catechism of the Catholic Church,* interestingly enough, underscores this truth: "The virtue of hope responds to the aspiration to happiness which God has placed in the heart of every man; it takes up the hopes that inspire men's activities and purifies them so as to order them to the Kingdom of heaven; it keeps man from discouragement; it sustains him during times of abandonment; it opens up his heart in expectation of eternal beatitude. Buoyed by hope, he is preserved from selfishness and led to the happiness that flows from charity."

"Where there is life there is hope," as the maxim has it. And where there is hope there is life. There is no stark choice between grace and nature, the theological and the anthropological. Grace affirms and brings to fulfillment what is natural. All creation is graced; the very "fallenness" of creation presupposes the grace of which sin is the denial. To be human is to live in hope, however vague and inchoate in our minds may be the object of that hope, or the reasons for that hope. *Homo viator* persists in believing that he is on the way to something, to somewhere; that there will be an arrival, somehow; and that, for the individual and the human project of which the individual is part, that arrival will vindicate the journey: It will not turn out, not finally, to have been either delusion or waste. It is the Christian proposal that this point of arrival, this home for the homeless, is ensured in the victory of Christ and the promise of his oncoming Kingdom. In the act of faith that is the acceptance of that proposal, the natural virtue of hopefulness becomes the theological virtue of hope.

There are very real alternatives to hope. The alternatives to hope are not just abstract possibilities but real-life options. To say they are options is to say that, in very important ways, they are subject to choice. They engage the will, the capacity to *decide* one way or the other. They are not just psychological states or personal dispositions built into our DNA. To believe that we have no choice is to succumb to determinism, and determinism is itself a form of despair. And despair is the first real-life alternative to hope. The second is presumption. Despair and presumption may appear to be opposites, but on closer examination, they are revealed to be two sides of the decision against hope.

Despair is to resign oneself to the suspicion—a suspicion that always hovers around the margins of faith—that the exile is permanent, that the hope of *homo viator* is a delusion. The dreamed-of, longed-for home is "pie in the sky in the sweet by and by." Perhaps death does have the last word. Despair may take the form of whimpering surrender, of fatalistic resignation, or of a brave "facing up to the facts." In its last form, it takes the stance of Stoicism, which is not without its moral dignity. Epicurus, the philosopher of Athens four centuries before Christ, gave classic expression to despair in the guise of unrelenting realism: "Death is nothing to us; for as long as we are, death is not here; and when death is here, we no longer are. Therefore it is nothing to the living or the dead."

Stoic resignation, which frequently presents itself as brave acceptance of the way things are, can also be an evasion of responsibility, a way of excusing one's complicity in the wrong of the way things are. Consider Hamlet's uncle, King Claudius. To Hamlet's grief over his father's death, Claudius says, "You must know, your father lost a father. That father lost, lost his."

Why should we in our peevish opposition
Take it to heart? Fie! 'Tis a fault to heaven,
A fault against the dead, a fault to nature,
To reason most absurd, whose common theme
Is death of fathers, and who still hath cried,

From the first corpse till he that died today,
"This must be so"

When Claudius speaks of "the first corpse," that would be Abel, of course, killed by his brother Cain. And Claudius, in order to gain the crown, killed his brother, Hamlet's father. In this case, as in cases beyond numbering, "This must be so" is not Stoic acceptance; rather, it is among the easy speeches that give false comfort to the guilty. It is frequently, and dishonestly, called "realism."

Despair can be sheer terror, or it can be philosophically construed as courage to face up to the way things are, or it can be contrived to excuse us from the judgment of what might be. We are not speaking here of disposition, but of decision. The subject is not deep melancholy or what today is called clinical depression. There are medical conditions requiring medical remedy. But there is also the danger of medicalizing the moral. A medical case study in senile dementia cannot, for instance, replace or "explain" the moral drama of *King Lear.*

In a religious context, despair is often discussed in terms of despairing of one's own salvation. The despairing soul believes that he is beyond forgiveness. He knows the parables of Jesus about the prodigal son and the lost sheep; he knows about the thief on the cross who, in the last gasping moments of a profligate life, asks for and receives the mercy of God. But none of this, the despairing soul believes, applies to his case. Thus does he decide against the mercy of God. And thus does he decide against the justice of God, who in Christ has borne the burden and the punishment of his sin. The word "decide" is from the Latin *decidere,* which means to cut off. One comes to a fork in the road, and to decide to go *this* way is to cut off the alternative of going *that* way. Despair is to decide against, to cut off, the mercy and justice of God.

The mercy and justice of God encompasses individual salvation but extends far beyond individual salvation. In the Book of Romans Saint Paul depicts the whole creation yearning for deliverance. Throughout these pages we have employed the biblical images of deliverance from slavery, return from exile, and *homo viator* in pilgrimage toward home. Personal salvation and cosmic salvation are inseparable. Personal despair of the possibility of forgiveness and salvation is of a piece with the denial of hope for the project that is God's creation. In philosophical language, it is the denial of the "final cause" or end (*telos*) of the creation that, Christians believe, has been vindicated in the death and resurrection of Christ. The realized fulfillment of that vindication is the Kingdom of God. The Kingdom of God is beyond the limits of what we call "history" and beyond the capacity of our imagination to envision. Here our most practiced language stumbles and stutters.

At the end of the Book of Revelation, the Apostle John was given a glimpse of what is to be:

> Then I saw a new heaven and a new earth; for the first heaven and the first earth had passed away, and the sea was no more. And I saw the holy city, new Jerusalem, coming down out of heaven from God, prepared as a bride adorned for her husband; and I heard a great voice from the throne saying, "Behold, the dwelling of God is with men. He will dwell with them, and they shall

> be his people, and God himself will be with them; he will wipe away every tear from their eyes, and death shall be no more, neither shall there be mourning nor crying, nor pain any more, for the former things have passed away."

And what about our personal experience of this cosmic transformation? John again: "Beloved, we are God's children now; it does not yet appear what we shall be, but we know that when he appears we shall be like him, for we shall see him as he is. And every one who thus hopes in him purifies himself as he is pure." To hope in him is to have faith in him, and to have faith in him is the present, albeit painfully provisional, *prolepsis* of what is to be. To despair is to decide against faith and hope.

Hope is faith disposed toward the future, and it is beyond doubt. The maxim of Cardinal John Henry Newman is well known: "Ten thousand problems do not add up to a doubt." It is a maxim often misunderstood. We all have the experience of uncertainty that is commonly called "doubt." It is an inescapable part of our searching and learning. But there is doubt, and then there is doubt. If someone promises that he is going to do a most extraordinarily difficult thing for you, you may experience uncertainty about how he is going to do it. That is one kind of doubt. Or you may say, "I doubt that you will do it." That is another kind of doubt. That is deciding against the promise. Despair is deciding, and deciding definitively, against the promise.

The other alternative to hope, presumption, also takes different forms. In terms of personal salvation, presumption is the belief that I pass muster more or less as I am and have no need for the mercy of God. "I'm OK—You're OK," to cite the title of a popular book of some years ago. Or at least I am, when compared to others, as OK as anyone, including God, can reasonably expect me to be. There was really no need for Christ to have gone to the bother of his death and resurrection. Not that I am anywhere near to being perfect, mind you, but a little tolerance for imperfection should be ticket enough for admission to whatever paradise is on offer.

Presumption is smugness, a supercilious complacency incapable of entertaining the thought either of final catastrophe, as in damnation, or of radical transformation, as in final glory. Presumption *presumes.* In another variation, it presumes on the mercy of God. The story is told of the Christian Gottlob Heine, the eighteenth-century classicist, that he was asked on his deathbed whether he was certain of the forgiveness of his sins. To which he is said to have answered, "Of course God will forgive me. That is his business." Much of Christian teaching and preaching in our time, pandering to the insatiable market for sundry forms of positive thinking and self-affirmation, majors in the sin of presumption. Presumption, like despair, is a decision against living in the promise.

Presumption as complacency is also so comfortably settling into our place of exile that we forget it is exile. It is the practical denial of the *status viatoris,* which, practiced long enough, may become a denial in principle. By virtue of the union of body and spirit, our experience is that of temporality, of "being in time." Conception, birth, growth, achievement, decline, death—we are creatures of time. The spirit cries out, "Home!" And the body makes it certain that time is the way toward home. The

Christian hope is not for escape from the body, but, as it said in the creed, for "the resurrection of the body." Time and eternity are not opposites, nor is eternity merely time without end. Eternal life is time fulfilled, beginning now in the life of faith disposed toward the future, which is hope.

In the existential philosophy of a Martin Heidegger, our existence is temporal both essentially and "in the foundation of its being." This is a necessary corrective to idealistic philosophies that invite us to rise to a God-like transcendence of our timed existence in history. Existentialism is right that we are creatures of time, but that does not explain our existence exhaustively and without remainder. Time, too, is a creature. There is reality "beyond time" to which our spirit bears witness. We are unable to conceive of reality beyond time because, being creatures of time, we are unable to think except in a temporal mode. It is an irrational presumption, however, to presume that reality is limited to what we can conceive.

Here again Josef Pieper makes an insightful connection: "Pride is the hidden conduit that links the two diametrically opposed forms of hopelessness, despair and presumption. At the nadir of despair, the self-destructive and perverse rejection of fulfillment borders on the most extreme form of the not less destructive delusion of presumption—the affirmation of nonfulfillment as though it were fulfillment." Think about it this way: In making the decision against the promise, which is despair, we are left with the intolerable thought that our existence is devoid of meaning. One remedy for this intolerable circumstance is to convince ourselves that, in our lives as they are, the promise has already been fulfilled, or is by our efforts in the process of being fulfilled, which is presumption. It is pride that links despair and presumption in denying that we are *homo viator,* living in hope of a destination that is not yet and will not be of our own achieving. It is, as we shall see, a pride that is not untouched by a measure of moral dignity.

Many people have written with wisdom on the subject of hope. In the second year of his pontificate, Pope Benedict XVI issued his second encyclical, *Spe Salvi.* In the Introduction to the encyclical, he refers to the Latin phrase *Spe salvi facti sumus* (In hope we were saved). The words are from Saint Paul in the Book of Romans. Benedict's first encyclical was *Deus caritas est*—"God is love." One might have thought from these titles that his program would be to address the three theological virtues—faith, hope, and love—in reverse order, and expected a third encyclical on faith. Benedict pointed, however, to biblical passages in which "faith" and "hope" seem to be used interchangeably. I have suggested earlier that hope is faith directed to the future. That is part of what Benedict was saying, but there is more to it than that.

He begins with a discussion of slavery and our experience of being enslaved to an unjust and intolerable present. In response to that circumstance, he says, "Christianity did not bring a message of social revolution like that of the ill-fated Spartacus, whose struggle led to so much bloodshed. Jesus was not Spartacus, he was not engaged in a fight for political liberation like Barabbas or Bar-Kochba." Barabbas, of course, was the prisoner released by Pontius Pilate in place of Jesus, and Bar-Kochba led the revolt of A.D. 132, ruling as king of Israel for three years before he and his people were totally crushed by the Romans. In Jesus, who himself died on a Roman cross, something very different appeared—"an encounter with the Lord of all lords, with the living God, and thus an encounter with a hope stronger than the sufferings of slavery, a hope which transformed life and the world from within." Benedict's aversion to liberation theologies, usually of a Marxist variety, is familiar, going back to his years as prefect of the Congregation for the Doctrine of the Faith, which is, under the pope, the chief doctrinal office of the Church.

In the nineteenth and twentieth centuries, for people beyond numbering, the Marxist scenario of revolutionary class struggle eventually leading to a "kingdom of freedom" was a hope not entirely unlike the Christian hope for the Kingdom of God. The collapse of that Marxist hope in our time has, it is not unreasonable to think, contributed in some circles to a fascination with catastrophe. There is a cultivated sense of doom in the face of environmental and other threats, each provided with dramatic depictions of Apocalypse Now—or at least apocalypse uncomfortably soon. But Benedict's is a more comprehensive point than the devastation of the Marxist hope: "Present society is recognized by Christians as an exile; they belong to a new society that is the goal of their common pilgrimage and which is anticipated in the course of that pilgrimage." In this society and in *any* society of historical time, the Church, meaning the Christian people, lives proleptically.

For most of human history, people have lived under the tyranny of various determinisms. The more sophisticated of the Romans had confined the gods and goddesses to the realm of mythology, removed from the events of history. They believed that events in the real world were in the control of cosmic forces that Saint Paul describes as "the elemental spirits of the universe." With the coming of Christianity, that form of determinism was broken. Gregory of Nazianzen in the fourth century offered the engaging suggestion that, at the very moment when the Magi, guided by a star, came to worship the child of Mary, astrology was finished. From that moment onward, the cosmos has orbited around the newborn king. That may strike us as a charming but fanciful image, yet it is closely related to the very serious claim that Christ is the *logos*—the word and the reason by whom all exists and to whom all is ordered.

Of course millions of people still consult the astrological prognostications published in the popular press, while many of the more thoughtful who scorn superstition offer their obeisance to different versions of "the elemental spirits of the universe." In this context, they are not usually called spirits, but evolutionary dynamics, life forces, or laws of nature. Yet these forces are just as impersonal as the stars. They work their inexorable ways in cold indifference to reason, to will, to love, and to hope. In short, it is suggested that the elemental spirits are in charge and that human freedom is a delusion, although a delusion hard to surrender, perhaps impossible to surrender. Remember thc philosophical proponent of materialistic determinism who is asked whether he believes in free will, to which he answers, "But of course. We have no choice but to believe in free will."

Despite all, we cling to the belief that we are unique persons, acting and hoping and aspiring in ways that have consequence, maybe even eternal consequence.

That belief is mocked by the elemental forces of determinism, and mocked unanswerably, or so it seems to many, by the reality of death. Posited against death's edict of ultimate meaninglessness, we unfurl the banner of hope for "eternal life." By eternal life Christians do not mean this life going on and on interminably. Benedict again: "To continue living forever—endlessly—appears more like a curse than a gift. Admittedly, one would wish to postpone death for as long as possible. But to live forever, without end, can, all things considered, only be viewed as monotonous and ultimately unbearable."

Some scientists today claim to be advancing what they do not hesitate to call "the immortality project." Life expectancy, they say, can be extended to 150 years, and then to 200, and then someday—why not?—500 years, and with no end in sight. Even a brief reflection on what this would mean for the relationship between generations and the increasingly desperate effort to sustain, in the relentless repetition of experience, a sense of purpose and hope might suggest that eternal life understood as interminable life would be more a curse than a blessing.

Eternal life is not this life continuing without end. Eternal life is the fulfillment anticipated by all that is good, true, and beautiful in this life. Eternal life is variously envisioned in different streams of Christian thought. One way of envisioning it is precisely as a vision, the Beatific Vision. The beatific vision is defined as the clear, unsullied, and eternally sustained vision of God in all his glory, which is to say, the full participation in the life of God who *is* goodness and truth and beauty.

This is beatitude, which means blessedness, which means holiness, which means wholeness, which means to be definitively, exhaustively, without remainder or qualification, *home.*

However far we stretch our imaginations, we can, at best, but touch on the penumbra of such a state of being. The eleventh-century Anselm of Canterbury said that God is that greater than which cannot be thought; likewise, the beatific vision of God is that greater than which cannot be envisioned. But most of us, and the great mystics more than most of us, have moments of encounter with the good, true, and beautiful in which we are moved to say, "Ah, it must be something like this." Recall again the words of Thomas Becket in Eliot's *Murder in the Cathedral:*

I have had a tremor of bliss, a wink of heaven, a whisper,
And I would no longer be denied; all things
Proceed to a joyful consummation.

In *Spe Salvi,* Benedict, who is very much an Augustinian, turns to Saint Augustine, who, in turn, turns to Saint Paul's observation in Romans that we do not know what we should pray for as we ought. Augustine writes, "There is therefore within us a certain learned ignorance." That is a suggestive phrase, *learned ignorance.* It is not only that we have learned this in the sense of having experienced that there is something within us that directs us to the desired unknown. It is also that the more "learned" we become, the more we reflect on this reality, the more we know we are entering ever more deeply into the unknown.

The Christian proposal is that in Jesus the unknown has made itself known in the finitude of space and time. Jesus says of himself, "I am the way, the truth, and the life." He is the human face of God. There is a wondrous phrase—*Finitum capax infiniti* (The finite is capable of the infinite)—that theologians have referred to in controversies over the Eucharist. In Jesus Christ, the infinite and the finite are one. If the infinite did not include the finite, it would not be infinite. In that case, what we call "the infinite" would be yet another finite thing, however great and glorious, because it would not include the reality we call "finite." But now God, the Infinite, has become a human being, so that, as the early fathers of the Church never tired of saying, we human beings may become God, meaning that we creatures will participate fully in the life of the Creator.

Jesus, crucified and risen in glory, and into glory, not only experiences the beatific vision; he *is* the beatific vision. But what does that say about that for which *we* hope? How does that help us envision the destination, the home, toward which our pilgrimage is directed? Again, the words of the apostle John: "Beloved, we are God's children now; it does not yet appear what we shall be, but we know that when he appears we shall be like him, for we shall see him as he is."

This claim is more than Becket's tremor of bliss and wink of heaven. In the opening words of the First Letter of John, the author can barely contain his excitement:

> That which was from the beginning, which we have heard, which we have seen with our eyes, which we have looked upon and touched with our hands,

> concerning the word of life—the life was made manifest, and we saw it, and testify to it, and proclaim to you the eternal life which was with the Father and was made manifest to us—that which we have seen and heard we proclaim also to you, so that you may have fellowship with us; and our fellowship is with the Father with his Son Jesus Christ. And we are writing this that our joy may be complete.

That astonishment of encounter and discovery, joined to the awareness that it creates a fellowship intended for all, is the reason why Christianity is an irrepressibly missionary faith. The Christian's joy is expanded in the expansion of the community of joy discovered. The pilgrim destination is not so much a place as a person. How do Christians envision their final return from exile? It is the personal encounter and eternal dwelling with one who is no stranger, for we knew him in his humility and will then see him in his triumph. The finite, once receptive to the infinite, is now received into the infinite. Received, not absorbed or subsumed, for we continue to be creatures, but now creatures perfectly attuned to the love by which and for which we were made.

The "eternal life" which we seek is not interminable life, but begins now in the encounter with the human face of God, Jesus Christ. The fulfillment of that life, described in biblical language as the Kingdom of God or the Kingdom of Heaven, is what Augustine elsewhere calls the "known unknown." This leads us to the *via negativa*—a way of knowing by what we do *not* know. The *via negativa* was powerfully inserted into Christian thinking by the fifth- or sixth-century writer "Pseudo-

Dionysius," so called because he was falsely identified with the Dionysius mentioned by Paul in Acts 17.

The *via negativa,* also called the *apophatic* way, arrives at positive truth about God by describing what God is *not* rather than what he *is.* So it is also with the ultimate hope proposed by Christianity. It is not *this* and it is not *that;* it is always the infinitely *more.* But always with this reservation: The infinitely more has been disclosed within the limits of *this* and *that.* Yet once again: "It does not yet appear what we shall be, but we know that when he appears we shall be like him, for we shall see him as he is."

The Christian hope is commonly expressed in terms of going to heaven when we die. This is not wrong, but it is woefully inadequate. It can induce a very constricted and individualistic idea of "salvation." Ours is a communal and corporate, indeed a cosmic, hope. In the New Testament, the Letter to the Hebrews repeatedly refers to our destination as a *city.* A city is not just a conglomeration of individuals but an intricately connected complex of patterns of association. The heavenly city is the New Jerusalem that stands in starkest contrast to our present life in Babylon. "Sin," writes Benedict, "is the destruction of the unity of the human race, as fragmentation and division. Babel, the place where languages were confused, the place of separation, expresses what sin most fundamentally is. Hence 'redemption' appears as the reestablishment of unity, in which we come together once more in a unity that is anticipated in the universal community of believers."

It is in this light of a future already happening that we understand the words of John: "That which we have seen and heard we proclaim also to you, so that you may have fellowship with us; and our fellowship is with the Father with his Son Jesus Christ. And we are writing this that our joy may be complete."

Redemption or salvation is thus viewed not as escape from this world but as participation in the future that is already happening in Jesus Christ and the community of faith in Jesus Christ. That participation takes the form of service to the world, a world that is the object of God's inexhaustible love. Among the best known of all biblical passages is John 3:16, "God so loved the world, that he gave his only Son . . ." While the New Testament sometimes refers to the *world* as that which is opposed to the world that God intends, such references have in mind a world that has turned against its own nature and destiny. Such a turn is evident in every manifestation of evil. It is also evident in the modern displacement of the gospel (the good news) of Christ with the gospel of historical progress.

When did that displacement happen and how? There are different answers to that question. In *Spe Salvi,* Benedict focuses on the influence of Francis Bacon, who is sometimes called the father of the scientific revolution. Bacon marks, says Benedict, "the new correlation of experiment and method that enables man to arrive at an interpretation of nature in conformity with its laws and thus finally to achieve 'the triumph of art over nature' (*Victoria cursus artis super naturam*)." The result is faith in progress, which, precisely as faith, has become something like a new religion.

Make no mistake about it: Benedict is not antiscientific or antimodern. Indeed, in his many statements on these questions, he is frequently near-rhapsodic in his praise of science and the achievements of the Enlightenment. Truth to tell, some who are sympathetic to his argument think he sometimes goes too far. In his commitment to the key modern values of reason and freedom, he expresses a sympathetic understanding of why the architects of modernity felt they had to throw off "the shackles of faith and of the Church" as well as the restrictions of the political structures of the period. Defenders of a premodern "Christendom" suspect he is altogether too sympathetic to those who felt the necessity of throwing off those "shackles." To speak of faith and the Church as shackles, however, is to speak of a historical distortion of Christian hope to which the anti-Christian forms of the Enlightenment were an understandable reaction. Benedict's argument is that, as with the distortion, so also with the reaction; it is now time to move on.

Benedict understands himself to be an apostle of reason and freedom, and also understands that reason and freedom are firmly grounded in the Western synthesis of Athens and Jerusalem. This, not incidentally, was the burden of his "controversial" lecture at Regensburg University in Germany on September 12, 2006, in which he raised the question of whether Islam can share the Christian understanding of the unbreakable connection between reason and the nature of God, and the related question of why violence in the name of religion is contrary to the nature of God.

There is no doubt that the key values of reason and freedom have contributed to what is rightly called "historical progress." But, as we discussed in Chapter 3, progress has definite limits, and at those limits it easily turns against itself in a fatal regression. At the height of its self-confidence, the Enlightenment envisioned infinite progress. Immanuel Kant, Benedict notes, wrote in 1792 that "the gradual transition of ecclesiastical faith to the exclusive sovereignty of pure religious faith is the coming of the Kingdom of God." Freed from the tyranny of the Church and of oppressive political systems, we are, wrote Kant, on the way to the home of our deepest longing.

A few years later, in 1795, Kant was having second thoughts. He then wrote: "If Christianity should one day cease to be worthy of love, then the prevailing mode in human thought would be rejection and opposition to it; and the Antichrist would begin his—albeit short—reign. But then, because Christianity, though destined to become the world religion, would not in fact be favored by destiny to become so, then this could lead, with respect to morality, to the perverted end of all things."

Kant and Nietzsche are philosophers of very different kinds, but both they and others were haunted by the thought that, once the Christian shackles were thrown off—if they could be thrown off—the result would be a new slavery to a power aptly described as "the Antichrist." One form of this new slavery is dramatically depicted by Nietzsche as the pitiful "Last Man," who, after the announced death of God, goes on about his business as though nothing has changed, as though there is no potency in pointlessness. The Last Man, like those described by the chorus in Eliot's *Murder in the Cathedral,* is "living, living, and partly living."

The hope without which we cannot live finds expression, again and again, in the idea of progress.

Progress depends upon freedom, upon imagination, innovation, and courage to act. The exercise of freedom involves beginning anew. The exhilarating idea of beginning anew, however, turns out to be a death sentence to the idea of historical progress. That is because there is no social order that, once achieved, is not, precisely because of freedom, subject to the next generation's beginning anew. Again and again in history, freedom is the undoing of freedom's achievement.

An obvious instance is the high culture of Germany. It is easily forgotten that, in the nineteenth and early twentieth centuries, Germany was the envy of the world. Its musical, literary, academic, and scientific achievements were the model emulated by all who embraced dreams of modernity. But, precisely because they were free, succeeding generations could and did bring it all crashing down in imperial warfare and the convulsions of the Weimar Republic, ending up in the moral abyss of Hitler and National Socialism.

But, one might argue, perhaps history could progress to the point where we create a social order that is not vulnerable to such tragic reversals, in which freedom is without risk. Returning to *Spe Salvi,* here is Benedict's response to that argument:

> Since man always remains free and since his freedom is always fragile, the kingdom of good will never be definitively established in this world. Anyone who promises the better world that is guaranteed to last forever is making a false promise; he is overlooking human freedom. Freedom must constantly be won over for the cause of good. Free assent to the good never exists

> simply by itself. If there were structures which could irrevocably guarantee a determined and good state of the world, man's freedom would be denied, and hence they would not be good structures at all.

To put it simply, the kingdom of freedom without freedom is not the kingdom of freedom. And, of course, were "progress" to reach such a terminal point, it would be the repudiation and not the fulfillment of the modernity project that is based on the rule of reason and freedom. Progress without the reasoned freedom to think and act is, in fact, regression to slavery. Against such delusory ideas of progress that end up by defining freedom as slavery and slavery as freedom, George Orwell wrote his classic dystopian tracts *Animal Farm* and *Nineteen Eighty-Four.* Similarly, the contemporary scientific ambition to "bring evolution under human control" must of necessity subject the future to the captivity of the present. In our mastery we are mastered.

We survey the history of the utopian dreams of the twentieth century in their real-life manifestations in communism and Nazism and draw back in horror from the unspeakable human cost exacted by making a religion of an idea of historical progress that is immune to the contingencies of freedom. Both communism and Nazism deemed millions of people to be expendable—whether Jews and Slavs or "counterrevolutionaries"—in the service of creating a new world, whether it be called the "kingdom of freedom" or the Thousand Year Reich. We must not think that the totalitarian catastrophes of that unhappy century are safely consigned to the past. The utopian impulse is deeply embedded in the human heart, and we can be sure that there is today a counterpart to Karl Marx working away in the British Library, or, more likely, in some biotech laboratory, contriving a plan for the creation of a home in history that will satisfy our longing for home.

There are, to be sure, more benign dreams of historical progress. Even if the new world of which we dream is not to be realized for generations to come, we may take some satisfaction in having contributed in some small way to its eventual arrival. But the actualization of that hope is always receding farther into the future; it is subject to ironic reversals beyond our capacity to anticipate; and, in any event, it is a hope for a future generation, not for me. I will die long before it is realized, if it is ever realized. Hoping in such a future is little more than leaving a greeting card for future generations, wishing them luck.

In our day many are gripped by apocalyptic scenarios of the future, whether in the form of global warming or other eco-catastrophes, or the end of human history in nuclear annihilation. Books appear with dependable regularity depicting a post-human future, some written in tones of deep foreboding, others taking grim satisfaction in Planet Earth's release from the scourge of humanity. In all these visions, there is no hope for the future vindication of the lives we have lived.

Turning away from such cosmic scenarios, people cling to the hope that they will live on in their children and grandchildren. When it comes to great historical figures such as Plato, Aristotle, or Abraham Lincoln, we speak of their living on, or at least of their spirit living on, in succeeding generations. "Now he belongs to the ages," declared Edwin Stanton upon the death of Lincoln. It is true that such figures are remembered by succeeding generations, but nobody today lives, or in the future will live, the life of Lincoln. Abraham Lincoln is dead.

So it is when, on a more modest scale, we speak of living on in our children and our children's children. If we mean by that the transmission of our genes, they are halved and halved again to the point of disappearance in a few generations. No rational person identifies future traces of DNA with the life that he has lived, with the person that he is. If we harbor the hope that someone in the future will live in acute and sustained awareness that he is, by virtue of biological connection, living our life, it is no more than a mean-spirited wish that that future person be denied the life that is his to live. Such callous desperation is repugnantly evident in popular fantasies about cloning. I may die but I will live on in my clone, or perhaps several clones. We frantically deny the undeniable fact that there will never be another "I" who, in the particularities of circumstance and experience, is the I who I mean when I say "I." With such brutal technological sophistication is egotism extended to the futile effort to create another to be the slave of our desire for perpetuity, of our denial of death.

The truth about life is that we die. We understandably protest the finality of that truth. We go not gentle into that night that seems anything but good. All our religion, our art, our poetry, our loves, our devotion to great undertakings, and not least the great undertaking of children and family, is a waving of little flags of protest against the finality of death. They are little flags of hope, without which we cannot live. "All serious and upright human conduct is hope in action," writes Benedict in *Spe Salvi.*

Benedict cites the Vietnamese martyr Paul Le-Bao-Tinh who in 1857 suffered unspeakable tortures before he was finally executed. During his imprisonment he wrote what Benedict calls "a letter from Hell," yet even in prison he rejoiced because he had hope. Benedict writes: "Christ descended into Hell and is therefore close to those cast into it, transforming their darkness into light. Suffering and torment is still terrible and well-nigh unbearable, yet the star of hope has risen, the heart, anchored in hope, reaches the very throne of God. Suffering does not cease to be suffering but, despite everything, becomes a hymn of praise." This is the heroic hope of the saints, grounded not in self-confidence but in identification with a narrative other than their own—the narrative of Christ crucified, risen, and returning in glory.

There continues to be an intense debate among Christian theologians as to whether God suffers. The normative account is that God is absolute Being and absolute Good and therefore "impassible," which means, among other things, incapable of suffering. But Benedict quotes approvingly the statement of Bernard of Clairvaux of the twelfth century: "God cannot suffer, but he can suffer with"—*Impassibilis est Deus sed non incompassibilies.* The Christian claim is that in Jesus, the Son of God and son of Mary, God assumed our human nature, did battle with every enemy of hope, suffered our death, and was raised triumphant. We shall overcome because he has overcome.

For those who do not accept the Christian reason for hope, it is still the case that "all serious and upright human conduct is hope in action." Nonbelievers have a "capacity to suffer for the sake of the truth," which, says Benedict, "is the measure of humanity." One can be grievously mistaken about the truth for which one suffers and nonetheless not be untouched by human nobility. Many suffered heroically for what they believed to be the truth of the Marxist promise. The great Alexander Solzhenitsyn writes movingly about the prisoners in the Gulag Archipelago who underwent excruciating torment and yet died in the belief that their unjust fate had contributed—somehow, they knew not how, they did not need to know how—to the realization of the just order promised by the Russian Revolution. Again and again they told themselves that, if only Stalin knew about the injustice they were suffering, he would set it right. But of course it was Stalin who was perpetrating the injustice. Their hope was not entirely unlike that of Job in the Old Testament, who said, "Though he should slay me, yet will I trust in him." Except, of course, that their trust was in an idol. Not for nothing was the classic book by disillusioned Marxists given the title *The God That Failed.*

In *Spe Salvi,* Benedict takes his argument in a direction that some may find surprising. He reflects on the significance of the Last Judgment, the belief that Jesus will return to judge the living and the dead. The Last Judgment, as depicted, for instance, in Michelangelo's magnificent Sistine Chapel, is intended to strike terror into the hearts of sinners. The message of the Last Judgment, however, is also a message of hope, says Benedict.

Contemporary atheism is in large part explained by the forgetting of that truth. Benedict writes:

> In the modern era, the idea of the Last Judgment has faded into the background; Christian faith has been individualized and primarily directed towards the salvation of the believer's own soul, while reflection on world history is largely dominated by the idea of progress. The fundamental content of awaiting a final judgment, however, has not disappeared: it has simply taken on a totally different form. The atheism of the 19th and 20th centuries is—in its origins and aims—a type of moralism; it is a protest against the injustices of the world and of world history. A world marked by so much injustice, innocent suffering, and cynicism of power cannot be the work of a good God. A God with responsibility for such a world would not be a just God, much less a good God. It is for the sake of morality that this God has to be contested. Since there is no God to create justice, it seems it is now up to man to establish justice. If, in the face of this world's suffering, protest against God is understandable, the claim that humanity can and must do what no God actually does or is able to do is both presumptuous and intrinsically false. It is no accident that this idea has led to the greatest forms of cruelty and violations of justice. This is grounded in the intrinsic falsity of the claim. A world that has to create its own justice is a world without hope. No one and nothing can answer for centuries of suffering. No one and nothing can guarantee that the cynicism of power—whatever beguiling ideological mask it adopts—will cease to dominate the world.

A world that has to create its own justice is a world without hope. . . . No one and nothing can answer for centuries of suffering. But here enters the astonishing claim that the God who is Love has in Jesus Christ volunteered to "answer for" the world's suffering and injustice. This he did in his death on the cross, a sacrifice of the infinite for the finite that is vindicated in his triumph over death. That vindication will be manifest to all at the Last Judgment, when absolute justice will be done with respect to all the evils of human history, and every wrong will be set right. "For this reason," says Benedict, "faith in the Last Judgment is the first and foremost hope. . . . I am convinced that the question of justice constitutes the essential argument, or in any case the strongest argument, for faith in eternal life." History cannot be set right within the limits of history.

Benedict alludes to Ivan's protest in *The Brothers Karamazov* that no final, eschatological outcome can justify the torture and death of even one child. Benedict agrees. "In the end," he writes, "evildoers do not sit at table at the eternal banquet beside their victims without distinction, as though nothing had happened." That would be yet another injustice, and an intolerable one. And yet, the God of justice is also the God of grace and mercy. It is not as though justice is "balanced" or "tempered" by mercy, as might be the case in a human court. Rather, the judgment of God—which infinitely surpasses but does not contradict our understanding of justice and mercy—does not only *include* both justice and mercy, but *is* both justice and mercy.

Admittedly, this explanation does not answer all our questions. But that is the way it is with realities that surpass our human understanding. Despite centuries of arduous effort by the greatest of minds, there is finally no intellectually satisfying answer to the question of theodicy—the question of how to justify to man the ways of God. There is the cross, the resurrection, and the promise that all will be set right. In this present exile before the fulfillment of that promise, there is the encouragement of Paul that we are to work out our salvation "with fear and trembling," in the knowledge and trust that at the final assize the judge is not only our defense lawyer, but the one who died that we might live.

Such is the hope by which Christians live. Pope Benedict's encyclical *Spe Salvi* is an intellectual tour de force and well worth reading in its entirety. His understanding of Christian hope and of atheism as a cry for justice is, I believe, something different in papal teaching. In this and many other writings, his sympathetic understanding of Augustine's view of the limits and possibilities of history, of the dialectic of time and eternity, of the conflict and intermingling between the city of man and the City of God, deserves to have a lasting influence on the way the Church proposes her faith to the world.

There are many thoughtful people who draw back from embracing that faith. They may have intellectual reasons for this, or they may simply misunderstand what Christianity proposes, or they may fear that making a commitment would mean a loss of the autonomy so prized in our culture. In the discussion of atheists and atheism in Chapter 4, I noted the presence among us of those who are called "atheists in good faith." They are called that not condescendingly but in genuine respect for their human dignity and, in most cases, their intelligence and goodwill.

The atheists I have in mind frequently prefer to describe themselves as "secularists" or as "secular humanists." Christians rightly lay claim to the title of humanism, pointing to a long tradition of great thinkers who are celebrated as Christian humanists, and noting that nothing could be more humanistic than the claim that God became a human being in Jesus Christ. But secular humanists, as that phrase is used today, are typically those who acknowledge no reality that transcends the *saeculum,* meaning the temporal order. In this view, all that was and is and is to be is confined within the limits of history. But do such humanists, *can* such humanists, live without hope? I doubt it.

Some kind of eschatology, a vision of what might be and perhaps will be, a sense of destination in which history culminates in the true community for which we long, is inherent in the thought and action of all serious people. Thoughtful secularists know that this longing, this presupposition of purposeful action, has again and again ended up in utopian irrelevance, chaos, or tyranny. They want no more of that. What then are they to do with this hope that will not go away and cannot be discarded without risking the loss of their humanity, and how are they rationally to explain it? Many invest their hope in historical progress, but I trust enough has been said on that score.

There are alternatives to investing one's life in hopes that may turn out to be delusory or lead to utopian fantasies that result in irrelevance, chaos, or tyranny. One may, for instance, hope to achieve what we may call "the satisfied conscience." People of strong moral convictions who, without explicit reference to religion, believe there is such a thing as moral law may find assurance that they have, all things considered, done what they ought to have done. By conforming to that moral law, they have given their lives something like an eternal validity.

This is a position that can be respected, even as one raises the question of whether it is not implicitly religious in character, for it contains unacknowledged assumptions about the purposefulness of history, a definitive judgment, eternity, and even a kind of salvation. Thoughtful people who adopt this view, however, insist that they are entirely secular. For such people, every life lived in faithfulness to moral truth is in itself an instance of history achieving its culmination. In his sympathetically critical treatment of this position, one philosopher describes it as a belief in an "inner-historical eschaton." Reality as a whole may have no *telos,* or final end, but every life lived well is a vindication of human hope.

Some who embrace this view understand themselves to be followers of Immanuel Kant, although that was not the view that Kant finally adopted. The idea that every good person is a kind of inner-historical eschaton does have a kinship with Kant's teaching that every person ought to be treated as an end and not merely as a means. It is something of a stretch, however, for the person of "satisfied conscience" to believe that his life answers the question of cosmic meaning. Such a view may reflect a modest opinion of history but an implausibly inflated opinion of the self. It implies an impossible disengagement of the self from the history by which the self is constituted and, however well intended, is not easily distinguished from egotism unbounded.

There is no vindication of the self in isolation from the world of which we are part. Again, the words of John 3:16—"God *so loved the world* that he sent his only Son . . ." (emphasis added). It is in the redemption of the world, not in disengagement from the world, that we seek our own redemption. In Christian imagery, that redemption of the world is the reversal of Babel's confusion of tongues, the Last Judgment of justice triumphant, the resurrection of the dead, and the correction and completion of all of history's distorted and defeated aspirations toward the good, the true, and the beautiful. It is the final deliverance from exile and arrival at the eternal home of the beloved community, the City of God at peace in the New Jerusalem.

Christians are those who have decided, and decided definitively, to settle for nothing less than that. Such is the teaching of Saint Paul in Romans: "We know that the whole creation has been groaning in travail together until now; and not only the creation, but we ourselves, who have the first fruits of the Spirit, groan inwardly as we wait for adoption as sons, the redemption of our bodies. For in this hope we were saved. Now hope that is seen is not hope. For who hopes for what he sees? But if we hope for what we do not see, we wait for it with patience."

We are not there yet. We are far from there. We are in a different place, a different point in time. We live in painfully partial and fragmented societies that are not authentic community. Our societies are riddled with conflicts and dualities, and permeated with deceptions and half-truths, the latter being the more vicious for the truths they distort. We cannot get beyond the dualities and conflicts that mock our yearning for authentic community: the dualities and conflicts of faith and reason, religion and philosophy, public and private, love and lust, the desire to serve and the ambition for power, the knowledge of what we ought to do and ought to be, and that knowledge at war with what we do and are. We are not transparent to one another. We are not transparent to ourselves. Community is communication, and our communication is clouded by deception and pretense, so that we do not know as we yearn to know, even about ourselves, what is true and what is false. We await the One who is the truth and who promised that the truth will make us free. We await in hope the time when we will know even as we are known.

Our present circumstance is profoundly, wrenchingly, unsatisfactory. Christian faith does not relieve but intensifies our dissatisfaction with things as they are. From all the centuries of exodus from slavery to freedom, from all the poor exiled children of Eve, the cry arises, "How long, O Lord, how long?" And with it the unceasing prayer of the saints, "Thy kingdom come, Thy will be done on earth as it is in heaven."

Skeptics and atheists may scoff at such hope, even as they grudgingly envy such hope. For they, too, hope. To live is to hope. To deny hope, to attempt to stifle hope, is radically false to human nature. Proponents of a "scientific" doctrine of materialistic determinism may depict themselves as Stoics bravely accepting the grim truth about reality, but they, too, are encountered by "signals of transcendence." In music, in nature, in laughter, in scientific wonder, and, above all, in love. They, too, protest wrong and condemn evil, implicitly recognizing that there is Right and Good by reference to which wrong is wrong and evil is evil. They, too, are possessed of an irrepressible intuition that all this is part of an infinitely greater More. They, too, ask in every present moment, "What next?" and know that the question is unending.

There is past and present and future, and what we call "present" is already past as quickly as we recognize it as present. We are creatures in time; our existence is timed; our experience bears witness to what might be described as the ontological priority of the future. The future is always presenting itself to us anew, having precedence, so to speak, over the past in the order of being. We live forward in time, radically entrusting ourselves to the Power of the Future who is God, and who holds together past, present, and future in the constancy of his love. Not a sparrow falling from the sky nor a hair from our heads will be lost, said Jesus. In response to which men and women beyond numbering have joined Julian of Norwich in her life's song of confidence in a final judgment by which all will be set right and "all shall be well, all shall be well, all manner of things shall be well."

A comforting delusion? We shall see in due course. But how desperate is the comfort drawn from belief in the obliteration of the self by death, in which case there will be no final accounting for our betrayals, our cruelties large and small, our deceits and acts of cowardice—all of which, it is hoped, will be consigned to oblivion. The hope that it does not matter, that *we* do not matter, may turn out to be the ultimate escapism, the ultimate evasion, the ultimate delusion.

It finally does come down to decision, to deciding for *this* and cutting off *that.* Decision is faith, a gift of grace. The person who seeks God and finds him, said Pascal, is both rational and happy. The person who seeks God and does not find him is rational but not happy. The person who does not seek God and does not find him is neither rational nor happy. Both rational and happy, we may add, is the person who in seeking discovers he is sought; who finds, in discovering, he is found. Hope reaches toward the future only to be surprised by the future in the present as revealed in the past. "Lo, I am with you always, even to the end of the age," said Jesus, and so, say Christians, he is and ever will be.

All human beings live in hope. The great difference is that the Christian declares a sure reason for hope. Peter counsels Christians to "always be prepared to give a reason for the hope that is in you," adding that they should do so "with gentleness and reverence." With gentleness and reverence, we are to offer our reason for hope to those who fight against the truth that they, too, live by hope.

Through the preceding chapters, these notes from exile have addressed various tasks of hope while living in Babylon. The life of faith has been depicted as a prolepsis of the promised New Jerusalem, the City of God in final tranquility. We examined the distinctively American understandings of life in exile, and the distinctively American ways of deluding ourselves that we have arrived home already. We celebrated progress, and we noted its sobering limits in the realm of morality.

We tried to engage the atheists among our fellow-exiles in this foreign city whose provisional peace we together seek. And also those who, like Richard Rorty, would distance themselves from hope's grief by means of liberal irony. In "Salvation Is from the Jews," we underscored the ways in which our pilgrim path and "the story of the world" are uniquely and inextricably entangled with the people of Israel. Then we explored the politics by which we alien citizens can ameliorate some wrongs and advance a provisional measure of the common good, even in Babylon. Finally, in this last chapter, we considered the impossibility of hopelessness and why it is that to live is to live in hope.

Throughout these pages, the proposal is that the whole creation groans for the glory that is to be revealed. With the resurrection of Jesus, a genuinely new world order has been inaugurated, and we are on the way, out from exile and on the pilgrim way toward the City of God. We are sustained on the way by faith's embrace of the presence in time of the End Time, who is the Alpha and Omega, the *logos* of all that has been, is now, and ever shall be. We are moving toward our destination, and our destination is moving toward us. At the very end of the very last book of the Bible are the words of Jesus, "Behold, I am coming soon." To which all the saints respond: "Amen. Come, Lord Jesus!"

As Christians and as Americans, in this our awkward duality of citizenship, we seek to be faithful in a time not of our choosing but of our testing. We resist the hubris of presuming that it is the definitive time and place of historical promise or tragedy, but it is our time and place. It is a time of many times: a time for dancing, even if to the songs of Zion in a foreign land; a time for walking together, unintimidated when we seem to be a small and beleaguered band; a time for rejoicing in momentary triumphs, and for defiance in momentary defeats; a time for persistence in reasoned argument, never tiring in proposing to the world a more excellent way; a time for generosity toward those who would make us their enemy; and, finally, a time for happy surrender to brother death—but not before, through our laughter and tears, we see and hail from afar the New Jerusalem and know that it is all time toward home.

Acknowledgments

This book is dedicated to James Nuechterlein, friend of long standing and editor of *First Things* over the first fourteen years of its publication. An inestimable debt is owed also to his successor, Joseph Bottum, whose wisdom and talent give me high confidence for the magazine's future. In the editorial office, I cannot imagine, and do not want to imagine, what we would do without my assistant, Davida Goldman, who was present at the creation. I am grateful to Denise Vaccaro for helping to maintain in the office a contagious spirit of disciplined work and cheerful fellowship. Mary Rose Rybak is a recently acquired treasure as managing editor. She is the one who, among other things, makes things happen on time. And, of course, Richard Vaughan, the business manager, who attends to circulation, fundraising, and other temporalities without which the magazine and other projects would be but another great idea. He, too, was present at the creation in 1990.

Each year we are blessed with the help of bright, determined, and devoted young people who serve as junior fellows and assistant editors. At the time of this book's publication, they are Stefan McDaniel, Ryan Sayre Patrico, Nathaniel Peters, and Amanda Shaw. My particular thanks to Nathaniel Peters for helping with notes and bibliographical details for this book. As with my last several books, it has been a pleasure to work with

Loretta Barrett, my agent, and Lara Heimert of Basic Books. To these and many others I am grateful for their contributions and trust they will not be embarrassed by their association with the argument of *American Babylon: Notes of a Christian Exile.*

Notes

Chapter I

6 **". . . abroad over the face of all the earth":** Genesis 11:1–9. With rare exceptions, biblical texts are quoted from the Revised Standard Version.

8 **"She who is at Babylon . . .":** 1 Peter 5:13.

8 **". . . exiles of the dispersion":** 1 Peter 1:1.

8 **"conduct yourselves with fear . . .":** 1 Peter 1:17.

8 **". . . wage war against your soul":** 1 Peter 2:11.

10 **"Babylon is the sphere . . .":** David Noel, ed., *The Anchor Bible Dictionary* (New York: Doubleday, 1992), 1:566.

12 **". . . seek the city that is to come":** Hebrews 11:37–40; 12:22–24; 13:14.

14 **"They shall hunger no more . . .":** Revelation 7:16–17.

15 **"I am the Alpha and Omega . . .":** Revelation 22:12.

16 **"Build houses and live in them . . .":** Jeremiah 29:5–7.

16 **"the wolf shall dwell with the lamb . . .":** Isaiah 11:6–9.

17 **"By the waters of Babylon . . .":** Psalm 137:1–6.

21 **. . . about a new beginning:** For a thorough discussion of the historical nature of the resurrection and its theological significance, see N. T. Wright, *The Resurrection of the Son of God* (Minneapolis: Augsburg Fortress, 2003), and Wolfhart Pannenberg, *Jesus: God and Man* (Louisville: Westminster John Knox Press, 1983).

21 **". . . by faith, not by sight":** 2 Corinthians 5:7.

24 **". . . any homeland is a foreign country"; "The soul is captive . . .":** "Epistle to Diognetus," in Bart D. Ehrman, ed., *The Apostolic Fathers*, vol. 2 (Cambridge: Loeb Classical Library, 2003), 121–160.

25 **"Whose minds went dark . . .":** "On Freedom's Ground," in Richard Wilbur, *Collected Poems* (Orlando: Harcourt, 2004), 120–121.

26 **. . . time toward home:** In 1976, I published a book by that title (*Time toward Home* [New York: Seabury Press]). My mind has changed about many things over the years, but not about the ways in which a "contract theory" of politics must be held in tension with a covenantal understanding of America in its founding and subsequent history.

Chapter II

27 **I once wrote a book . . .:** *Time toward Home* (New York: Seabury Press, 1976).

27 ***Time* magazine did a long report . . . :** "Again, God's Country," *Time,* October 20, 1975.

28 **"identity kit":** Personal conversation with Peter Berger, although the essential idea is suggested in his book, with Thomas Luckman, *The Social Construction of Reality* (New York: Anchor, 1967).

29 **"universal nation":** See Ben Wattenberg, *The First Universal Nation* (New York: Free Press, 1992).

30 **"the story of the world":** Robert Jenson, "How the World Lost Its Story," *First Things,* no. 36 (October 1993): 19–24.

32 **. . . are intermingled:** St. Augustine, *City of God,* Book XIX, Chap. 27.

32 **"Seek the welfare of the city . . .":** Jeremiah 19:7.

32 **"culture warrior":** Eric Gregory, *Politics and the Order of Love: An Augustinian Ethic of Democratic Citizenship* (Chicago: University of Chicago Press, 2008).

33 **"The Roman Empire has been shaken . . .":** St. Augustine, *City of God,* Book IV, Chap. 8.

33 **"It is beyond anything incredible . . .":** Ibid., Book V, Chap. 12.

33 **. . . achievement of that place and time:** Oliver O'Donovan, *The Desire of the Nations: Rediscovering the Roots of Political Theology*

(New York: Cambridge University Press, 1999); Oliver O'Donovan, *The Ways of Judgment: The Bampton Lectures, 2003* (Grand Rapids, Mich.: Wm. Eerdmans, 2005).

33 **"doing ethics for Caesar":** This is a favored phrase of Duke University theologian Stanley Hauerwas. Robert Louis Wilken, "A Constantinian Bishop: St. Ambrose of Milan," in *God, Truth, and Witness,* edited by L. Gregory Jones, Reinhard Hütter, and C. Rosalee Velloso Ewell (Grand Rapids, Mich.: Brazos Press, 2005), 78.

34 **"The adjustment of the relation . . .":** A. D. Lindsay, *The Modern Democratic State* (Oxford: Oxford University Press, 1942), 60.

35 **. . . treatise of 1594 . . .:** Richard Hooker, *Of the Laws of Ecclesiastical Polity,* edited by A. S. McGrade (Cambridge: Cambridge University Press, 1989).

35 **"errand into the wilderness":** Perry Miller, *Errand into the Wilderness* (Cambridge: Belknap Press of Harvard University Press, 1956).

36 ***America's Theologian:*** Robert Jenson, *America's Theologian: A Recommendation of Jonathan Edwards* (New York: Oxford University Press, 1992).

36 **"Tis not unlikely":** Jonathan Edwards, quoted in Thomas S. Kidd, *The Great Awakening* (New Haven, Conn.: Yale University Press, 2007), 158.

37 **. . . the cosmic story of salvation:** The story of how that confidence has worked its way through history is brilliantly told by Ernest Tuveson in *Redeemer Nation: The Idea of America's Millennial Role* (Chicago: University of Chicago Press, 1968).

38 **"the American religion":** Harold Bloom, *The American Religion: The Emergence of the Post-Christian Nation* (New York: Simon and Schuster, 1993).

39 **. . . the national founding:** See Michael Novak, *On Two Wings: Humble Faith and Common Sense at the American Founding* (New York: Encounter Books, 2001); James H. Hutson, *Religion and the*

Founding of the American Republic (Washington, D.C.: Library of Congress, 1998).

39 **"naked public square":** Richard John Neuhaus, *The Naked Public Square* (Grand Rapids, Mich.: Wm. Eerdmans, 1984).

43 **"wanted [their] utopian America . . .":** Richard Rorty, *Achieving Our Country: Leftist Thought in Twentieth-Century America* (Cambridge: Harvard University Press, 1998).

44 **"veil of ignorance":** John Rawls, *A Theory of Justice,* rev. ed. (Cambridge: Harvard University Press, 1999).

45 **H. Richard Niebuhr:** *The Kingdom of God in America* (Middletown, Conn.: Wesleyan University Press, 1988).

45 **. . . some of his critics:** For a vigorous, even harsh, criticism of Reinhold Niebuhr, see Stanley Hauerwas's Gifford Lectures, *With the Grain of the Universe: The Church's Witness and Natural Theology* (Grand Rapids, Mich.: Brazos, 2001).

48 **Reinhold Niebuhr:** *The Irony of American History* (New York: Scribner, 1985); *The Children of Light and the Children of Darkness* (New York: Scribner, 1972).

49 **" . . . hatred and vainglory":** Niebuhr, *Irony,* 174.

50 **. . . unavoidable point of reference. . . :** John Courtney Murray, *We Hold These Truths* (Lanham, Md.: Sheed and Ward, 1986).

53 **Lippmann's proposed remedy. . . :** Walter Lippmann, *The Public Philosophy* (New Brunswick, N.J.: Transaction, 1989).

CHAPTER III

64 **. . . moribund or dead:** Robert Nisbet, *History of the Idea of Progress* (New Brunswick, N.J.: Transaction, 1994).

66 **"the artist's accession . . .":** Quoted in ibid., 343–344.

66 **" . . . envy future generations":** Quoted in ibid.

67 **" . . . the brain may not be capable . . .":** Quoted in ibid., 344.

71 **" . . . meaningless history of the Greeks":** Reinhold Niebuhr, *The Nature and Destiny of Man: A Christian Interpretation,* vols. 1 and 2 (New York: C. Scribner's Sons, 1941–1943), 1:24.

72 **"... no solution of its own problem":** Ibid., 2:154–155.

73 **"... history is not its own redeemer":** Niebuhr, *Nature and Destiny*, 2:206.

73 **"... things in heaven and things on earth":** Ephesians 1:9–10.

77 **"the philosopher from nowhere":** Richard John Neuhaus, "A Curious Encounter with a Philosopher from Nowhere," *First Things*, no. 120 (February 2002): 77–82.

79 **"What matters [now] is the construction . . .":** Alasdair MacIntyre, *After Virtue* (Notre Dame: University of Notre Dame Press, 1st ed. 1981; 3rd ed. 2007).

83 **"... the same as not to see":** C. S. Lewis, *The Abolition of Man* (New York: HarperOne, 2001).

84 **"... freedom's possibility":** Pope Benedict XVI, Encyclical Letter *Spe Salvi* of the Supreme Pontiff Benedict XVI to the Bishops, Priests, and Deacons, Men and Women Religious, and All the Lay Faithful on Christian Hope, http://www.vatican.va/holy_father/benedict_xvi/encyclicals/documents/hf_ben-xvi_enc_20071130_spe-salvi_en.html, 2007, section 24.

Chapter IV

88 **"the sacred canopy":** Peter Berger, *The Sacred Canopy: Elements of a Sociological Theory of Religion* (New York: Anchor, 1990). See also Peter Berger, "Secularization Falsified," *First Things*, no. 180 (February 2008): 23–27.

92 **everyone who thinks is a believer:** Michael Polanyi, *Personal Knowledge: Towards a Post-Critical Philosophy* (London: Routledge, 1962).

93 **"... individual men in their solitude":** William James, *The Varieties of Religious Experience: A Study in Human Nature* (New York: Signet Classic, 2003), Lecture 2.

93 **"the naked public square":** Richard John Neuhaus, *The Naked Public Square* (Grand Rapids, Mich.: Wm. Eerdmans, 1984).

94 **"... the guardians of belief":** James C. Turner, *Without God, Without Creed: The Origins of Unbelief in America* (Baltimore: Johns Hopkins University Press: 1986).

100 **MacIntyre's criticism . . .:** Alasdair MacIntyre, *Three Rival Versions of Moral Enquiry: Encyclopedia, Genealogy, and Tradition* (South Bend, Ind.: University of Notre Dame Press, 1991).

104 **" . . . God has to be contested":** Pope Benedict XVI, Encyclical Letter *Spe Salvi* of the Supreme Pontiff Benedict XVI to the Bishops, Priests, and Deacons, Men and Women Religious, and All the Lay Faithful on Christian Hope, http://www.vatican.va/holy_father/benedict_xvi/encyclicals/documents/hf_ben-xvi_enc_20071130_spe-salvi_en.html, 2007, section 42.

105 **" . . . an atheism of sorrow or of expiation":** Cantalamessa, quoted in "The Public Square," *First Things,* no. 179 (January 2008): 64–64.

106 **"Promises, covenants, and oaths . . .":** John Locke, *A Letter concerning Toleration,* 1689.

106 **" . . . the claims of Civil Society":** James Madison, *Memorial and Remonstrance,* 1785.

110 **. . . vibrantly alive . . .:** James Hutson and Jaroslav Pelikan, *Religion and the Founding of the American Republic* (Washington, D.C.: Library of Congress, 1998).

110 **. . . spelled out in illuminating detail . . .:** See Michael Novak, *On Two Wings: Humble Faith and Common Sense at the American Founding* (San Francisco: Encounter Books, 2002).

111 **. . . elements of the Deist vocabulary:** George McKenna, *The Puritan Origins of American Patriotism* (New Haven, Conn.: Yale University Press, 2007), 45ff.

Chapter V

120 **" . . . anticipated in the course of that pilgrimage":** Pope Benedict XVI, Encyclical Letter *Spe Salvi* of the Supreme Pontiff Benedict XVI to the Bishops, Priests, and Deacons, Men and Women Religious, and All the Lay Faithful on Christian Hope, http://www.vatican.va/holy_father/benedict_xvi/encyclicals/documents/hf_ben-xvi_enc_20071130_spe-salvi_en.html, 2007, sections 2 and 4.

120 **". . . a bond like siblinghood . . .":** Augustine Thompson, *Cities of God* (University Park: Penn State Press, 2005), 311.

124 **"The great religions of antiquity":** Peter Gay, *The Enlightenment: An Interpretation* (New York: W. W. Norton, 1967).

125 **"Augustine read Paul and Plotinus . . .":** Robert Wilken, "Who Will Speak *for* the Religious Traditions?" *Journal of the American Academy of Religion* 57 (1989): 699–718.

126 **. . . synthesized with Reformation Christianity . . . :** Henry F. May, *The Enlightenment in America* (New York: Oxford University Press, 1976).

126 **Scottish Enlightenment:** Alasdair MacIntyre, *Whose Justice? Which Rationality?* (South Bend, Ind.: University of Notre Dame Press, 1988).

127 **Rorty's proposal:** All following quotations from Rorty come from *Contingency, Irony, and Solidarity* (New York: Cambridge University Press, 1989).

130 **". . . overflowing with sheer self appreciation":** Georges Bernanos, *The Diary of a Country Priest* (New York: Carroll and Graf, 2002), 22.

130 **. . . ideas pertinent to a just polity:** Richard Rorty, *Objectivity, Relativism, and Truth* (New York: Cambridge University Press, 1991), 175–196.

132 **". . . Shall we judge reality . . . ?":** Etienne Gilson, *Thomist Realism and the Critique of Knowledge,* translated by Mark A. Wauck (Ft. Collins, Colo.: Ignatius Press, 1986), 169.

145 **. . . optimistic view . . . :** This is evident in, among other writings, *Achieving Our Country: Leftist Thought in Twentieth-Century America* (Cambridge: Harvard University Press, 1998).

147 **. . . death and suffering beyond measure:** Simon Schama, *Citizens: A Chronicle of the French Revolution* (New York: Vintage, 1990).

147 **. . . massive study of rescuers . . . :** Samuel P. and Pearl M. Oliner, *The Altruistic Personality* (New York: Free Press, 1992).

152 **"Rawlsian searchers for consensus . . .":** Richard Rorty, *Objectivity, Relativism, and Truth,* 21–34.

Chapter VI

164 **"Woman, believe me . . .":** Jesus' conversation with the woman at the well appears in John 4:4–30.

165 **"A point of departure":** F. F. Bruce, ed., *The International Bible Commentary* (Grand Rapids, Mich.: Zondervan, 1986), 1468.

166 **"how the Johannine Jesus . . .":** Rudolf Bultmann, *The Gospel of John* (Louisville: Westminster John Knox Press, 1971), 189–190.

166 **" . . . unique privilege be thereby dissolved . . .":** C. K. Barrett, *The Gospel according to John* (Philadelphia: Westminster Press, 1978), 198.

167 **"God has not rejected his people . . .":** *A Select Library of the Nicene and Post-Nicene Fathers of the Christian Church,* edited by Philip Schaff, vol. 7, *St. Augustin: Homilies on the Gospel of John; Homilies on the First Epistle of John; Soliloquies.* (New York: The Christian Literature Company, 1888; reprint, Peabody, Mass.: Hendrickson, 1994), 101, 106.

169 **"the story of the world":** Robert Jenson, "How the World Lost Its Story," *First Things,* no. 36 (October 1993): 19–24.

170 **"Remember not the former things . . .":** Isaiah 43:18–19.

172 **. . . Christ is the cornerstone:** Ephesians 2:20.

173 **"But if some of the branches . . .":** Romans 11:17–20.

173 **" . . . even as we are known":** 1 Corinthians 13:12.

173 **" . . . This stranger who resists . . .":** Quoted in David Novak, *Jewish-Christian Dialogue: A Jewish Justification* (New York: Oxford University Press, 1992), 106.

175 **. . . anguished ponderings . . .:** Paul's discussion about the Jews is in Romans 9:11. The doxology is found in Romans 11:33, 36.

176 **"plurality and difference . . .":** Christopher Leighton in *Christianity in Jewish Terms,* edited by Tikva Frymer-Kensky (Boulder: Westview, 2000), 47–48.

177 **" . . . Abraham's stock":** "Declaration on the Relationship of the Church to Non-Christian Religions" (*Nostra Aetate*), no. 4.

178 **" . . . a question to be left to the Holy Spirit"; "I want to thank the Pope . . .":** H. H. John Paul II, *Crossing the Threshold of Hope* (New York: Knopf, 1995), 99–100.

179 **" . . . trustees of the promise . . .":** *Catechism of the Catholic Church*, no. 60.

179 **"How many thousands . . .":** Acts 21:20.

180 **" . . . promised redemption is surely yet to come":** Novak, *Jewish-Christian Dialogue*, 155–156.

181 **" . . . such the Father seeks to worship him":** John 4.4–30.

181 **"And I saw no temple . . .":** Revelation 21:22–26.

CHAPTER VII

184 **"For now we see in a mirror dimly . . .":** 1 Corinthians 13:12.

184 **" . . . the way, the truth, and the life":** John 14:6.

185 **"a number of citizens, . . .":** James Madison, *The Federalist*, No. 10.

187 **"locked in civil argument":** John Courtney Murray, *We Hold These Truths* (Lanham, Md.: Sheed and Ward, 1986).

193 **"The meaning, content, and foundations . . .":** United States, President's Council on Bioethics, *Human Dignity and Bioethics: Essays Commissioned by the President's Council on Bioethics* (Washington, D.C.: U.S. Independent Agencies and Commissions, 2008), 13.

193 **. . . keenly aware that their goal . . . :** Mary Ann Glendon, *A World Made New: Eleanor Roosevelt and the Declaration of Human Rights* (New York: Random House, 2001).

207 **. . . stem-cell research . . . :** Maureen Condic, "What We Know about Embryonic Stem Cells," *First Things*, no. 169 (January 2007): 25–29.

208 **"This reductionist dream . . .":** Thomas Nagel, "The Fear of Religion," a review of Richard Dawkins's *The God Delusion*, in *The New Republic*, October 23, 2006.

209 **" . . . legal ideas uncolored . . .":** Oliver Wendell Holmes, "The Path of the Law," in *Collected Legal Papers* (New York: Harcourt Brace, 1920), 179.

Chapter VIII

213 **"It was one of those mysterious fairy calls . . .":** Kenneth Grahame, *The Wind in the Willows* (New York: Sterling, 2005), 61–62.

214 **"By the waters of Babylon . . .":** Psalm 137:1, 5–6.

215 **" . . . the greatest of these is love":** 1 Corinthians 13:13.

215 **"It would never occur to a philosopher . . .":** Josef Pieper, *On Hope* (Ft. Collins, Colo.: Ignatius, 1986), 25.

216 **"Hoping against hope . . .":** Romans 4:18.

216 **"Although he slay me . . .":** Job 13:15.

217 **" . . . happiness that flows from charity":** *Catechism of the Catholic Church,* 1818.

218 **" . . . peevish opposition . . .":** *Hamlet,* Act I, scene 2.

220 **. . . yearning for deliverance:** See Romans 8:18–23.

221 **" . . . the former things have passed away":** Revelation 21:1–4.

221 **"Beloved, we are God's children . . .":** 1 John 3:2–3.

223 **" . . . in the foundation of its being":** Cited in Pieper, *On Hope,* 16.

223 **"Pride is the hidden conduit . . .":** Ibid., 61.

224 **In hope we were saved:** Pope Benedict XVI, Encyclical Letter *Spe Salvi* of the Supreme Pontiff Benedict XVI to the Bishops, Priests, and Deacons, Men and Women Religious, and All the Lay Faithful on Christian Hope, http://www.vatican.va/holy_father/benedict_xvi/encyclicals/documents/hf_ben-xvi_enc_20071130_spe-salvi_en.html, 2007. All quotations from Pope Benedict XVI in this chapter are from this encyclical. The phrase "in hope we were saved" is in Romans 8:24.

226 **"the elemental spirits of the universe":** Colossians 2:20.

228 **. . . we do not know what we should pray for . . . :** Romans 8:26.

229 **" . . . the way, the truth, and the life":** John 14:6.

230 **" . . . our joy may be complete":** 1 John 1:1–4.

239 **. . . whether God suffers:** See Thomas Weinandy, "Does God Suffer?" *First Things,* no. 117 (November 2001): 35–41.

240 **"Though he should slay me . . .":** Job 13:15.

243 **"with fear and trembling":** Philippians 2:12.

245 **"inner-historical eschaton"; "the satisfied conscience":** Glenn Tinder, *Liberty: Rethinking an Imperiled Idea* (Grand Rapids, Mich.: Wm. Eerdmans, 2007), 363 ff.

246 **" . . . wait for it with patience":** Romans 8:22–25.

246 **"signals of transcendence":** The sociologist Peter L. Berger examines "signals of transcendence" in his book *A Rumor of Angels: Modern Society and the Rediscovery of the Supernatural* (New York: Doubleday, 1969).

249 **"Lo, I am with you always . . .":** Matthew 28:20.

249 **" . . . a reason for the hope that is in you":** 1 Peter 3:15.

250 **"Behold, I am coming soon":** Revelation 22:20.

Index